Starseed

A Quest to Embrace One's Inner
Light and Overcome the Shadows
of Dysfunction, Abuse & Fear

DR. STACEY LAMAR

STAR IN THE LOTUS

Published by:

Star in the Lotus

NEW YORK

www.thesource-ny.com

ISBN: 978-1-7357730-0-1

Editing: Kathleen Barnes
Cover & interior design: Gary A. Rosenberg

Printed in the United States of America

*This book is written with gentleness and love for
each Starseed that has chosen a path of healing as
an incarnate human. It is dedicated to their work
in Light and to all the Angels and Spirit guides
that have protected them during their journeys.
The work is challenging and at times feels futile,
but it is the Grace of the Divine that sustains them.
This book is attuned in Light and offers validation and
peace to all that receive the message with an open heart.*

Contents

Preface

The life of a human Starseed is not easy to say the least. This soul is naïve and bursting with unconditional love and compassion.

To manifest as a human filled with desire to heal others is a daunting task that is often underestimated in the depth and volume of challenges that await. A natural healer and many times a natural leader, the Starseed will choose a family that is dysfunctional and wrought with challenges prior to conception. These challenges I will refer to as "Shadow" throughout this book. Dysfunction, abuse in many forms, manipulation, and other negative behaviors are complex Shadows that are often intertwined.

For example, exposure to alcoholism in a family is commonly associated with coexisting emotional and/or physical abuse. Being born into poverty comes with a host of emotional and physical challenges such as low self-esteem and the statistical likelihood of remaining in poverty. Shadow is not limited to individuals and families. Properties, communities and societies can be impacted by the Shadow of the energy that surrounds them, the result of years of negativity manifesting in that region.

Today's political climate which includes dishonesty, divisiveness, racism... speaks to the overwhelming Shadow in the U.S.

that is energetically felt by the multitude. This societal Shadow can make Starseeds more susceptible to fatigue, depression, anxiety, and other physical and emotional symptoms.

Not all humans are Starseeds and not all Starseeds are consciously aware of their souls' identity.

Religion and modern science have remained conflicted on the existence of a higher power for thousands of years. Reliance on these perceived higher authorities weakens one's ability to access personal intuition, that little voice within that warns of danger and assures of safety. It is almost a "use it or lose it" phenomenon resulting from deferring personal power to the organization of choice. The long-term result is a feeling of disconnectedness between self and Spirit. Yet, over time religious and scientific oppositions may be the spark that begins the search for the deeper meaning of self for the Starseed. Controversies and conflicting doctrines simply cannot align with the soul of a Star and the search for "who am I" becomes renewed. This sparks a new quest for true purpose, revealing the core belief that we are not alone as we seek to connect with the Universal Spirit. The awakening of human consciousness begins and the journey of Starseed reveals.

Not all humans originate from Star energy and not all humans choose Light. Free will mandates personal choice for each soul in human form. Although other human forms are respected and acknowledged, this book is written to validate the Starseed. It is this soul energy that frequently chooses a unique and difficult path in human form with the intention of helping others and to be of service in some manner. Starseeds who self-identify with coming from Light often describe their early human beginnings as difficult, toxic even abusive. A deep and heavy Shadow is the earliest teacher of true human suffering for the Starseed. They must work to overcome personal adversity and assimilate the lessons. They often turn to religion or science during this process as a means to define or put into context, but it often falls short. They are left feeling empty or with the feeling that something is missing. Deep within they know *there is more* and that *they are more* but cannot explain why they feel that way. There is an innate connection to greatness of the universe and profound appreciation for the uniqueness of even the smallest creature. It is not until Shadows are identified and the lessons revealed that then the Starseed's Light begins to shine. The Light shines and the journey of healer begins.

This book offers validation to the Starseeds seeking understanding of their personal suffering, knowing it is with purpose. The Shadow experienced, the lessons revealed, and the shining of your Star Light will empower you to be the healer you are meant to be. Keeping in mind that healers will always face Shadows. No human is immune to suffering, but as a Starseed, you will be better prepared to follow through with your life's purpose and positively impact other souls. This book shares stories from other Starseeds and outlines steps to heal, protect, and empower yourself as you remain committed to your true life's purpose.

—Stacey

CHAPTER 1

The Starseed Defined

There is no scientific definition, measurable, quantifiable or peer-reviewed to describe a Starseed. Research today is reliant on the Internet search which brings a multitude of information from un-vetted websites that publish opinion and definition based on whatever subject they are trying to purport.

So, what is a Starseed? Simply put, a Starseed is any human who believes in a soul originated from a distant Star system. This generates the appreciation that the human self has a soul housed within. It also implies the belief they are human and soul, a belief that is rooted in faith. Although it has been theorized that Star energy may be within the DNA, to date this has not been proven.

Yet, isn't that typical for any esoteric concept? This book is not written to challenge science or religion. The personal conviction of any person that they are *more than* human is imprinted in their soul and immeasurable, unprovable, and deserving of respect for their individuality.

Self-identification is front and center at this time as different genders and ethnicities refuse to be labeled within a few limiting categories they assert do not resonate with them. This issue has triggered chaos in many traditional institutions of democracies. Political and health-based systems are struggling to re-define what it means to *self-identify*.

Self-identification is to "*assign* a particular characteristic or categorization to oneself; describe oneself as belonging to a particular category or group." (https://en.oxforddictionaries.com/definition/self-identify).

The language of complex surveys to simple patient demographic forms has been rewritten to demonstrate sensitivity to *self-identification*. This has created ethical debates that include validity and when have we gone too far. I bring this up because the same arguments can be made for those awakening humans that are beginning to grasp that they are more than human. The karmic imprint of the soul is awakening and Starseed humans are changing how they *self-identify*. Science hasn't caught up with them yet, the consideration that Star energy being within DNA is not implausible.

Religion may be supportive within the subscribed doctrine, but the Starseed often feels incomplete within a traditional institution. I will take it one step further and state that to many Starseeds organized religions do not resonate with their souls because they do not feel authentic to the message from the God Source. This statement will send the devout into a tailspin. It is not intended to dismiss religious institutions outright.

Yet, speak to Starseeds who have experienced one religion or another and they will share their distrust in the veracity of the doctrine and often the leadership of the institution. The suggestion that many religious texts have been altered over time has been corroborated by theologians for decades. As for distrust of leadership, distant and recent history has plenty of evidence to support corruption and cover up of financial and sexual indiscretions in more than one of the primary faiths.

But this book is not intended to disparage religions or to conduct a post-mortem of religious doctrine or legal misappropriations. It is intended to define and celebrate the Starseed. And for Starseeds, early exposure to religion may be the catalyst for further seeking their true identity. As they awaken and their Light shines brighter, they begin to feel less connected to their tribe, i.e. religious belief system or human family. Long periods of disconnectedness can lead to repression of their true feelings and the sequalae of depression, loneliness and other physical symptoms. These symptoms will persist until a spark presents and they begin to believe they are not alone. Until this time, the Starseed just exists.

Today's spirituality, metaphysical and esoteric concepts are categorized in the New Age system. This is problematic since there is nothing "New" about our souls and the infinite karmic imprint that has stood the test of time. However, if you are seeking information regarding spirituality outside of tradition then it is within New Age teachings that most will generally begin.

I cannot stress enough that since these concepts are wrought with differing opinions and lack credible science, it is imperative that you tap into your higher self (intuition) vs your lower self (ego) to differentiate your truth. The abundance of false information can mislead the seeker and derail from their personal truth. The best guidance I can offer is if it feels wrong, then it is likely wrong. The Divine does not want to mislead or cause fear, but unfortunately many Dark energies that work to counter the Light do. This is the duality of our existence. Walking in the Light, we must differentiate and navigate through Shadow as part of our growth and development.

CHAPTER 2

Born in the Shadow

My journey in this lifetime begins with organized religion seeking to derail my existence from the moment I took my first breaths in a small community Catholic hospital. My Mother retold our story many times from as early as I can remember. It may very well had been a bedtime story since it is etched so prominently in my mind. I wasn't more than five years old when I learned that my birth wasn't planned. The story went that my mother became pregnant by my father on her 18th birthday. She would revisit her painful memories of my grandfather's shame and condemnation of her when he learned his daughter was unmarried and pregnant. She spoke of the punishments my grandfather imposed and how he kept her hidden in her bedroom for months. She was forbidden to leave the house when she was pregnant for fear that she would be recognized by people he knew.

My birth was not a proud and celebrated moment. It was the 1960s and, as I learned, the nuns who operated the labor floor at the hospital worked tirelessly to try to convince my mother to give me to them. My mother described how the nuns didn't want her to hold me or be with me in the hospital. They believed it would be best that way. I have no doubt the nuns believed they were doing God's work, that children born out of wedlock were "bastards", shunned from society. But my mother did keep me, for better or worse, and my parents married the month following my birth. Was this my first encounter with Shadow seeking to prevent me from experiencing my intended soul's journey or a failed attempt of the Light trying to intervene from the pain to follow?

I was three years old when my mother was said to have "snapped". It followed my sister's birth and was most likely undiagnosed post-partum depression, but that didn't exist in textbooks back then. Post-partum depression a devastating diagnosis likely contributed to the chain of events that followed, however, in reality, my mother could not cope with her life. She gave up. She didn't try for the good of her children. She went from doctor to doctor and was given prescriptions for anti-anxiety medications. They gave her pills and she slept all day. All day, every day, my mother slept.

Her way to cope was to sleep and when she was awake, she behaved like a manipulating child herself. Her manipulative behavior gave her freedom from raising a family, without the shame of admitting that she just didn't want to be a mother.

Dysfunction could have found its definition in our household in the early 1970s: A mother who spent every day impaired by Valium and a father who avoided reality by spending his days in isolation in the basement of the duplex home where we lived. My father had created a workspace in the basement that became his sanctuary from the irrational, manipulative woman he had married. He would leave us and hang out with his pot-smoking friends whenever the opportunity arose.

One of my strongest recollections of that time is my fear that he wouldn't return from these jaunts and my sister and I would be left alone with our mother. Before my mother's illness, my father was a blue-collar worker. He worked with a local union, but his job ended suddenly when my mother became extremely fearful of being left alone and he could no longer leave her side to fulfill his work obligations.

With no household income, poverty quickly fell upon us and we were supported through food stamps and family charity. Shame and embarrassment were compounded since we lived in a small town where privacy was compromised by small town living.

To call my mother abusive would be an understatement. The only childhood memories I have involve some form of emotional or physical abuse by her and my father rushing in to protect me. My mother's favorite form of punishment for me was beatings with the buckle end of a thick leather belt. She was merciless. With no tolerance for common childhood behavior, my mother would "fly off the handle bars" for the most trivial occurrences. Accidentally spilling a drink, leaving the front door open, not going to bed precisely on time were all fair game to my mother to grab the belt and induce fear, shame, and physical pain on my being.

There were many occasions that I went to school wearing a plain Catholic school uniform that covered welts from the punishment of the preceding evening. But, I would pretend all was well, as I laid the foundation for my life by wearing a mask that made me "normal."

I recall many nights sleeping in the same bed with my little sister (we didn't have separate beds) with her rubbing my hair as I cried. She would tell me I would be okay. My 4-year old sister would comfort me, the older sister, and try to make my pain go away.

It wasn't just physical pain that I endured. The emotional trauma seems even more damaging as I attempt to recover. One of my earliest memories was being told that my father might not really be my father. When my mother became angry she would find it necessary to share with me that it was "possible," depending on her mood sometimes it was "likely," that my father was not truly mine. So, in addition to the physical torment came the emotional turmoil of planting doubt in my only childhood certainty, my father.

My sister and I were cocooned by dysfunction, phobias, and abuse that wore us down from our earliest memories. We knew our lives were different than those of our friends, but we couldn't grasp the depth of wrongness. We never had sleepovers with friends. We never had play dates at our house. We left for school in the morning and pretended to fit in with our classmates. When we returned home to our reality, our pretend normalcy was left on the other side of the door to be reclaimed on another day.

Of the two of us, I was labeled the "difficult" child. My sister was much more passive and agreeable. She was better able to avoid causing the disruptions that so upset my mother. I was more active and more challenging. My mother interpreted my youthful energy and curiosity as being "difficult." Looking back on it, I guess I was "difficult" because I was unable to be a passive participant in my life or give my childish permission for my mother to sleep the days and weeks and months away in a state of emotional numbness.

So, I endured the physical beatings, the welts, and even a broken toe while my mother failed to cope. I became her punching bag, the target of all of her frustrations. I'm an adult now, but up until I reached the age of 40, when I recalled these events, I could still feel the shame and pain of an innocent child, deep within my soul.

I spent my entire childhood accepting the label of being "the difficult child." I felt sorry for my mother and blamed myself for her problems. I believed that if only I hadn't been born, she could have had a better life. The story of my unwanted conception had been shared with me enough times that clearly my mother wished I had never existed. I believed I deserved her punishments. I was bad. I was worthless. Yet, every once in a while, this little voice would whisper within me that I was so much more. That I was important. That I was good.

The only love I knew came from my father. I clung to him and was sent to terror when I didn't know where he was. He gave me sympathy and protection from my mother. He tried hard to compensate for her abuse and make me feel loved. He took his own abuse from her in the process. He succumbed to his own anxiety during these years, himself a victim of mistreatment and suffocation caused by my mother's manipulative behavior.

My parents' negative behaviors seemed to feed off each other and their fears and anxieties were synergistically fueled. The more debilitated my mother became, so did my father. They evolved into two phobic, crippled people who were incapable of providing a healthy nurturing environment for their children. It was inevitable that anxiety and fear would attach themselves to my sister and me. My best memory of my early childhood is I have no best memory. Our home had no feeling of love, comfort or happy within its walls. The Shadow was heavy and dark. The sadness was its own life form. It fed off the suffering of each of us and if I couldn't learn how to persevere, I would surely lose my Light.

This was my dysfunctional beginning with my soul-crippling label of "difficult" by the Mother who was supposed to nurture. Reading this story, it is easy to brand me "victim" as it is commonly believed that children have no say in the family they are born into. They didn't ask to be put into bad circumstances; therefore, they are victims.

For me, victim doesn't resonate. My little voice always told me I had purpose. I innately believe God doesn't make mistakes. Therefore, could it be that each soul chooses to be born into a specific family for a specific reason? I accepted challenges within this family of souls, so that I could grow and develop into the healer I am meant to be. I'm not a victim, but a student of suffering, learning valuable lessons in my soul's evolution.

Next, let's substitute different terminology to describe the events of my childhood. Abuse, dysfunction, fear... and let's substitute the term "Shadow" as we re-frame events into the duality of Light and Dark.

Yes, my childhood sucked. I was drowning in a family life of addiction, fear, child abuse and poverty. I prayed to God for better days and clung to faith that I was important and that I did matter. Each of my parents struggled in their roles because neither of them was prepared to parent, nor did they want to be married. The negativity that was the cloud of despair clung over each of us, despair that was the result of the karmic imprint of souls within that family dynamic. Each person within this cloud entered in human form with a mission and purpose, but not each soul had intentions that were Light. It was the blending of the karma of these four souls in my family that contributed to the patterns that were created. It became a war of Light versus Dark as each soul revealed the goodness or badness within.

From the age of 5, I knew I was not bad, despite my mother's insistence. I knew I had a bigger purpose for being born. I believed in God. I believed in Angels. I believed in helping others. I had all the prerequisites of the incarnate Starseed years before my spark occurred. I was hungry for guidance, but first had to overcome the darkness that was my foundation. It was all part of my Divine growth and development. It was through my pain that I would develop empathy. It was through personal judgement that I would choose not to judge. It was through overcoming Shadow that my Star energy would shine. But it would be decades before this revelation would take place. Many years of suffering remained, and painful lessons Divinely designed to empower my soul and serve to heal others.

CHAPTER 3

Living with
the Darkness

My parents separated when I was ten. Living with my mother was not an option and my father struggled to keep his sanity and find any work he could do to feed us. We were soon homeless and with only one option. Living with my aunt, my father's sister, was that option.

Living with family should seem reasonable during tough times and certainly by most would seem safe. But, in the family I was born into, a darker family you would not meet.

We shared one room, my father, sister and I, in three twin beds in a small attic room. After a few weeks of witnessing me being emotionally tormented by my aunt, my sister begged to go live with my mother. My mother was living in a one-room studio apartment in a motel next door to my grandparents which for her was the lesser of the two evils we were given. I had no choice. My mother abandoned me, despised me, and referred to me as "your problem" when speaking to my father. There was no way I would survive living with our mother again. I would rather run away and live homeless than spend another bitter night with her. I would try to fit in with my aunt's family. I knew it was going to be difficult, but I would try to keep my distance and just focus on my studies.

We lived with my aunt for several months before my father was able to find us a new family member to spend time with. During these months I was called names, shamed for expressing concern or interest in when my dad would return home and generally ridiculed for anything my aunt chose to make fun of. In the beginning, she hid her disdain with a false face of concern she wore in my father's presence. But as months passed, her ability to hide the abuse was less of a concern and her true dislike of me became evident.

The long-term effect of living with this abuse was crippling fear when I did not know where my father was and when he would return. I would shake. I would cry. I would pace. These are, of course, all signs of what might be considered PTSD today. My panic was the result of a horribly insensitive abusive woman who enjoyed belittling others regardless of their tender age.

It's funny when we look in retrospect at the world we have experienced, how keenly the adult mind processes memories a child's mind cannot comprehend. Today, I refer to this time of my childhood as living in the Darkness but will even be bolder as to say I was living with Dark entities. Demon, reptilian, vampire? I am not going to presume to know, but I will say that if asked during my childhood to describe the environment during this time, I would liken it to living in a dark room where the lights are never turned on. And what is the consequence of being surrounded by darkness? Science supports that light deprivation is related to depression, mood disorders, sleep disorders... For me, I was living in a cruel and emotionally unsafe space, a spiritual darkness, once again with people that I was supposed to trust. Yet, these people enjoyed witnessing human suffering.

They were aware of the pain they caused and made it a point to criticize and belittle me for expressing fear.

The only positive influence during this time of my life was that I was able to excel academically. The Darkness could not stop my success in school although I was frequently taunted for being book smart. My books were where I found refuge until my father could find a safer place to reside. Nearly a year passed, and we did find an affordable apartment. My father worked hard to provide and my sister remained with our mother.

My teenage years provided a bit more stability with my father working and a safe home, but I never experienced maternal support. Feminine milestones like menstruation and puppy love were to be learned by myself. Mom and daughter lunch dates or shopping sprees were things I longed for, even envied, however never experienced.

I struggled with my self-esteem. In my teen years, I bounced from boyfriend to boyfriend searching for a normal relationship and a normal existence. I never shared my private experiences with anyone. Dysfunction, phobias, and abuse were my secret life concealed within my soul and masked by my façade.

My father tried to fill both roles, mom and dad. I am grateful for his love and support as he was struggling through his soul's journey. He set a personal standard impossible to meet. But try he did, with sincerity and genuine love. Money was always a concern, our life was modest, but I was never without his simple wisdom and support. Wisdom that remains timeless and lessons that I've shared with many young people during my professional career.

"The sky is the limit," he said. "Follow your heart. Be true to yourself, and most importantly, always be able to provide for yourself."

He added, "Never ever rely on a man to support you. Be able to take of yourself, just in case things don't work out."

This was sound advice from a loving father who spent every day just trying to survive for his daughters.

My dad remains challenged even today by his personal demons. His life remains modest. Low self-esteem and alcohol addiction continue to challenge him as he advances in years, but his heart has remained full of love and support. He never walked away. God knows it would have been easier for him if he did.

The horrible suggestion that my father is not truly my father has continued over the decades. My mother brought it up again as recently as a few years ago, despite adamantly denying its veracity for the previous 40 years. Thus, it is very possible that my father and I may not be biologically connected. But, the answer will remain unknown for the time being.

I believe there is a price to be paid for holding on to Dark secrets for decades. Suppression of shame, guilt, and lies can manifest into illness of body, mind, and spirit. My once beautiful mother's health has systematically declined overtime and from my perspective much of her pain is self-induced. Perhaps the result of the shame of creating a family life based on her willingness to deceive. Creating a Shadow of deception. Using manipulation as a means of control over souls that you are supposed to lead can backfire and cause personal harm.

Illness such as *Agoraphobia* plagued my mother from my earliest memories. Victims of this disorder frequently are unable to leave their homes and suffer with a pathological fear of open spaces and being alone. My mom has struggled with this fear and subsequent addiction for decades. She has had moments of strength and years where she was functional, but this is unsustainable because of the Shadow of fear which she cannot overcome despite all available community resources.

She did eventually remarry, a man she met through a dating service. My sister and I knew it wasn't a relationship built on love and respect; rather it was another attempt to find someone to take care of her. That marriage failed when she once again fell into the repetitive patterns I remember from my childhood, sleeping all day, addicted to pills and living a life of dysfunction.

When I'm in my mother's presence, the pattern of my childhood repeats itself. I can feel illness such as nausea, fatigue, and sadness attempt to repossess my physical being. The Shadow that is my mother has strength. It has clung to her and consumed her energy to the point where she cannot function as an independent being. It is heavy. I don't feel Light in her presence. There is no happy, joy, or love around her. Yet, I LOVE MY MOTHER! I love her for the soul she is and for the suffering she experiences. I remain sad that her soul has not evolved because I am aware of all the opportunities that she had. Yet, I have learned on my spiritual path that not all souls are Light and not all souls will stay Light. Life is hard!

Each journey is challenged with ups and downs and not everyone is going to succeed. With my mother, her Shadow doesn't like my Light and when Dark symptoms try to manifest within my being it is time for me to distance myself. I send love and prayers but acknowledge that I must detach from the energetic cords that want to drain Light from within me. In the past, I interpreted her fear as manipulation and a way to deflect personal responsibility from decisions that she really did not want to make. As my journey has progressed along with my deeper understanding of mission and purpose, I now appreciate that my mother didn't fail me or my children. My mother has only failed herself. It was in my mother's mistakes where my deepest lessons lie about what not to do and who not to be. My choice to incarnate with this family provided me opportunity to navigate through Shadow's that overtake many souls so that I could better appreciate suffering and healing.

The most difficult lesson to date is having to accept that each soul has to make their own choices. I cannot stop the suffering for anyone including mom, dad, sister, or child. I can only lead by example. I can share my suffering and my healing processes. This along with daily prayers is where the Starseed is most impactful.

CHAPTER 4

The Power of Fear

A foundation of fear in the developmental years left unresolved will inevitably carry into adult life. Early triggers become imprinted in our existence and, though they may lay dormant, they are not healed. In my life, the extreme emotions that came with persistent dysfunctional patterns resulted in an adulthood largely consumed by being fear. Fear of loss, fear of failure and fear of abandonment travelled with me each day despite my best efforts to shed them. Despite my best efforts to shed my fear or at least put on my daily mask of normal, each day brought an internal sense of waiting for the next tragedy to occur. My human body lived in a perpetual state of fight or flight, readiness for battle. This sense of fear carried with me through most of my young adulthood and manifested in endless choices that were my attempts to normalize my dysfunctional existence.

After elementary school, I convinced my father that I really wanted to go to a public high school. I think he was relieved deep down since he would now be released from the burden of figuring out how to pay for my next four years. I did okay in public school. I was a regular teen girl and I felt like I "fit in." I was surrounded by all colors and social classes, so I didn't stand out in the crowd.

I stopped going to church regularly, but I still believed in God. I believed I was watched by my own guardian angel and this internal belief kept me tethered to religion during different parts of my journey. I trusted that my life had a "higher purpose" despite not really being able to define what that meant to an adolescent. Sure, I partied and took risks like most teens, but by sixteen years old my focus returned to God and faith. My personal struggle with my identity led me to the Evangelical church of my first "real" boyfriend. My first heartbreak when our love wasn't going to be forever. A mutual friend invited me to attend a Christian concert where I met Gavin and the new romance believed to be Divinely inspired. Gavin, from the South, was part of the musical group that was performing in my area. We connected instantly and the long-distance courtship lasted about a year and was quickly followed by marriage. One month before my 18th birthday I said "I do" and hitched a ride south to escape the pain of old memories wrapped up in a belief this marriage was what God intended. The church elders had blessed this marriage so I trusted they must know. Yet, something felt quite wrong. I recall the drive along the interstate days after the wedding, knowing that this was a mistake. Unfortunately, I didn't have the courage, or the family role models, to discuss how I felt. I just sat quietly in the car listening to the tires gently thump along the road, watching the mile markers change as we passed through each new state on the way to a fresh start. My new home. New beginning. New nightmare.

Suffice it to say this decision was destined to fail. Sadly, I had no thoughts of furthering my education or planning my future. My family never discussed travel abroad, college, or career. My only positive role models were the church elders who believed I was in a blessed marriage. They encouraged the idea and I desperately needed an exit from my existence. I saw no future. I could not envision that I was better than this choice. My esteem was grounded in feelings of inadequacy and not being wanted in the first place. My birth was a mistake. To have someone want to marry me might be my only path to escape. Fear of not being wanted the key motivator to my ultimate failure. Innocent belief that God wanted me to marry this man helped me to speak the vows, but crippling fear came over me the day the car drove out of my familiar world into the vast unknown.

The roller coaster ride commenced with the marriage vows. It only took a few weeks to identify the gravity of this mistake, but I worked to make a new life down south for about a year. Gavin travelled for work, so he was away several weeks a month. I was 18 years old, alone, and just trying to figure out what to do next. I waited tables and took a course to become a travel agent. As the end of year one approached, I finished travel agency coursework and longed to return home. I realized that I am a Northern gal. New York is my home and where I longed to be. It took a few weeks of courage to let Gavin know I was going to return home. My fatal mistake in that conversation was offering for him to join me. I did not think he would accept, but he did.

Our return to New York just prolonged the inevitable. I tried to love Gavin and I tried to make the marriage work. If for nothing else then to avoid the cutting "I told you so" that was expected by my mother, who was incapable of empathy. For more than five years I rode this roller coaster and periodically would try to get off. Each time Gavin would beg me to stay, renounce divorce as sin, and guilt me till I gave up and conceded to forever.

I began to expand my thoughts on my future and what did I really want to be when I grew up? I continued in the travel industry for a few years, but this was unfulfilling, so I returned to community college to earn a degree in nursing. My fifth year of marriage brought many changes. I completed my nursing degree. My first son was born. I was growing and maturing and beginning to resent Gavin more each day for not allowing me to leave a loveless marriage that should have never happened. But, for the sake of my son, Devin, I was determined to keep trying. He deserved a foundation of love with role models to provide guidance, structure, and support. I owed him that. For one year more I tried to remain in a loveless marriage, becoming more resentful of Gavin each day and feeling guilty that I could see no future for myself or my son in this environment. This was not a healthy family unit. Gavin's manipulation worsened with Devin's birth. Unfortunately, my son became the pawn Gavin needed to punish me for leaving.

The dissolution of our marriage should have been uncompli-cated. No property owned. No assets to distribute. Shared custody of one minor child. In New York State, a straightforward process, uncontested and mutually planned. But Gavin was unwilling to accept the failure and determined to control the narrative. An ending that was a painful and protracted drama that scarred many souls. The pain was felt by many, the lessons learned by few.

CHAPTER 5

Abducted

I remember it like it was yesterday.

I left for work one Friday evening in the fall of 1990, shortly after I had told Gavin I was leaving. At the time, I was working the night shift from 11 p.m. to 7 a.m. so I would be home with Devin during the day. Many nurses choose this path when they're raising small children. This type of scheduling flexibility is one of the appeals of being a nurse. About 20 minutes after I started my shift that night, my father arrived on the hospital floor. He was frantic. Dad had been staying with us for a few weeks and when he returned home, he discovered a most distressing scene.

Dad was shaking as he tried to explain to me that Gavin's sister and her boyfriend were at our apartment with a rental truck and they were packing up Devin and all his belongings and leaving. He had tried to call me from our apartment, but Gavin in a rage pulled the phone from the wall and broke it. There were no cell phones in 1990. In a panic to reach me, my father rushed to my workplace to tell me that my son was being taken away.

We left the hospital immediately. It took no more than 30 minutes for my father to arrive at the hospital, explain the situation to me and for us to return to my apartment. But it was too late. The apartment was empty. Gavin had taken my son, his belongings and most everything he could pack in a hurry. The only thing that remained was Devin's antibiotics in the refrigerator. He was being treated for an ear infection at the time. I was consumed with fear. This was not in *my* plan.

I called the police. I called my sister. I called my attorney. Reports were taken, but we had no idea which direction they were headed. To further fuel my panic, the police could not file a kidnapping report because Devin was with his father. Gavin could technically take our son anywhere he wanted since we were married and no separation agreement had been signed. Therefore, the police couldn't stop him. It was out of their hands. With those words, I felt the breath leave my body.

By that time, it was the early morning hours of Saturday. My attorney told me that my hands were tied over the weekend until Monday morning when we could schedule an emergency hearing with the family court judge. Gavin had planned well by waiting for a weekend to take my son. This was certainly not a plan that he would have concocted on his own. Someone had counseled him on this choice.

I am at a loss for words to describe the fear, physical pain and heartbreak that I felt the moment I realized my son was missing. I had no idea which direction on this Earth they were heading and I could do nothing to rescue him before Monday morning. I felt dead. My existence would end until I had Devin back.

Time literally stood still that weekend. Over and over, I called Gavin's parents begging and pleading for information about my son. All weekend long, they calmly denied they knew anything and continually hung up on me. Then they would take the phone off the hook for several hours so I would get an endless busy signal.

The very first time I called was certainly the most memorable. Gavin's father answered the phone. His voice was icy cold and full of hatred. I heard a combination of anger mixed with his personal victory as I begged for answers as to the whereabouts of my son. The monotone Southern accent was full of bitter smugness when he answered, "I have no idea what you are talking about," followed by, "You're as good as dead in Devin's eyes now, so why don't you just move on?"

I think at that very moment all blood left the top half of my body and rushed to my feet. I went limp as I realized that these people, Gavin's family, were planning on keeping my son forever. The phone line went dead, but those words in that evil voice replayed in my head over and over and over again.

Nearly thirty years later, I still hear those words in my head with the same intensity of evil and hatred whenever I think of that moment. By the end of that and many other desperate phone calls to my in-laws, I began to feel certain that Devin was on his way down South to Gavin's hometown. I knew I was in for a battle.

I stopped eating the night Devin was taken. I couldn't sleep. All I could do was scream and cry all weekend long. I did take occasional sips of water at the urging of my father and sister. I knew that if I ended up in the hospital I might never get him back, but food was out of the question.

Monday morning finally came. I met with my attorney very early to prepare for an emergency hearing with the family court judge I came to know as Judge H. When Judge H. heard our problem, he immediately ordered Devin's return to his home county. The only problem was that we had no idea where Devin was. This was the million-dollar question. More accurately, the $15,000 question because, in 1990, that is what it cost for me to locate my son and get him back.

Here is a brief history lesson about 1990. There was no Amber Alert, back then, nor was America's Most Wanted televised in my area. The police were completely unhelpful and unsympathetic. The police advised me that Gavin did not break the law because Devin was his son, too. Thank God for the compassion of Judge H. who became instantly agitated and joined my mission to bring my son home.

But where was Devin? The next step was to hire a private investigator. My attorney recommended Mr. Franklin to help find them and get Devin back. The going rate was about $500 a day. I was 24 years old, desperate and not able to afford that kind of money. I thought I was doomed. Fortunately, my grandparents lent me a few thousand dollars and the search began.

Somewhere between Monday morning and Tuesday morning after a few hundred calls to my in-laws' house, Gavin finally answered the phone. It was this moment that confirmed their location and the rescue operation could begin. Gavin told me that Devin was fine and how he tells stories to him about me every day and shows him my picture.

"Oh, my God!" I thought. "This guy has lost his mind."

I was losing it, too. In that brief conversation, I begged Gavin to bring Devin home. I begged him to not hurt Devin this way. I said anything I could think of to appeal to his son's best interest. It was like speaking to a stone. He hung up on me. I knew I had to get to that town quickly and get my son back.

I recounted the bizarre conversation with Gavin to Mr. Franklin and my attorney and explained Gavin believed that he was going to keep me from my son and raise him as if I was just a memory.

Armed with the court order, Mr. Franklin began to prepare to travel to Gavin's hometown to retrieve my son. Judge H.'s order for Devin's return was in compliance with the Interstate Child Protection laws that were in place. Gavin's home state was one of many that had signed this agreement, so the law demanded that the child be returned to the state in which he resides. Therefore, Mr. Franklin expected this order would be upheld by this Southern state without delay.

I had a sinking feeling he was going to be wrong. I insisted I travel with Mr. Franklin, so we bought two airline tickets South. Upon our arrival, we rented a car and headed into the small town where Gavin was raised and Devin was being kept. Population 900, maybe.

Mr. Franklin maintained that my son's transfer was going to be uneventful. The two states involved both had allegiance to the Interstate Child Protection Act and there was a responsibility upon those states to honor court orders.

Wrong! Little did we know that Gavin had reported to the local authorities that I was a child abuser and he was fleeing our home in search of protection. With his allegation, my clear-cut case instantly became mud. I was now a perceived child abuser and the local authorities were looking to arrest me. Yes, arrest me! I was in a very bad predicament. I was exhausted, starving and frantic as all these events started to unfold.

By the time Mr. Franklin came to the realization that we were getting the runaround from the local police, it was nightfall of Tuesday evening. Devin had been missing for four days. I was closer to him geographically, by distance, but still impossibly far from any resolution. It was the end of Day Four and I still didn't have my son.

To protect my anonymity, we secured hotel rooms approximately 25 miles from Gavin's hometown. Mr. Franklin was quite fearful that I might be arrested on a phony charge. He called Judge H. at home and advised him of what we were up against. From what I was told, Judge H. was very angry. He asked for

27

the local judge's name and phone number and planned on calling him directly the next morning.

I recall Mr. Franklin trying to comfort me before I went to sleep. He wanted me to stop worrying about the money it was going to cost for him being on the job for several days. He was very compassionate and promised that it was his goal to return my son to me even if I couldn't pay. Mr. Franklin was enraged that local officials would be deceptive and dishonor an agreement between states designed to avoid issues like the one we were facing. I appreciated his kindness, but I didn't feel comforted.

Early Wednesday morning, I learned that Judge H. had spoken with the Gavin's local community judge. I also was dismayed to learn that Judge H. was getting the same runaround that we were. I knew I had to do something and I knew I had to act fast. Mr. Franklin and I drove to the local courthouse to continue the futile journey of getting my son back through the legal process. He instructed me to stay in the car, lock the doors and duck down so I wouldn't be recognized. Mr. Franklin remained fearful that if I was identified in this town I would be arrested on a false charge. I promised to comply and stayed out of sight as Mr. Franklin locked the car doors and headed for the courthouse. The events that followed happened so quickly that all communication between Mr. Franklin and I ended until late the following day. No opportunity to explain my actions in private to Mr. Franklin ever emerged.

I was locked inside the rental car and obeying Mr. Franklin's instructions. As I stayed hidden beneath the view of passersby, I periodically peeked my head up in search of any sign of my son. In one of my brief moments gazing out the car window, I spotted my husband and father-in-law driving right past the courthouse. Gavin parked in front of a building a few hundred feet away and across the street. My mind raced! How could I just sit and hide when they were right across the street? I had to do something.

I had to speak with Gavin. I couldn't trust the legal system anymore. It was Day Five and my son was no closer to me than the first day he was taken by his vengeful father. The legal papers that were supposed to secure my son and return him to his home were no more valuable than the paper they were written on. I was from the North. Gavin was from the South, from the Deep South to be more precise. This was clearly a different world. This town was not just fighting me; it was still fighting the Civil War.

I had known for several years that the locals in Gavin's community did not much care for him marrying a "Northern gal." But this took it to a whole new level of contempt. So, I did it. I got out of the car, walked across the street, and entered the building my husband was in. It turned out to be his lawyer's office and I was standing square in front of the secretary. I calmly requested to speak with Gavin. She advised the lawyer that I was there and then directed me to his office. There I saw Gavin and his father sitting in front of the desk of a middle-aged dark-haired man wearing wire-rimmed glasses.

I asked to be allowed to speak with Gavin and his lawyer, outside of the presence of my father-in-law. The lawyer accommodated my request and that moment I became an actress. I did not speak one honest word, but I was the most desperate and believable, empty soul that would do anything in my power to get my son back. I did just that. I gave up my soul, my integrity, and part of my innocence to reclaim my son. I have no regrets.

I began the conversation with Gavin and his attorney by

telling them how sorry I was for this big misunderstanding. I told them both how much I loved Gavin and how I was mixed up and sorry for the undeserved pain that I caused him.

I explained that this was a family issue that needed to be resolved privately and not in the court system. Gavin's lawyer, of course, agreed and began quoting Bible references about marriage. After a little time passed, I asked if I could please speak with my husband privately. The attorney agreed this was a good idea and Gavin recommended we take a short drive to talk. I agreed and we headed about a mile out of town. Gavin parked the car. Within five minutes, we were having sex in the front seat as I proved my undying love for him.

It was vile. I felt like a whore. With each disgusting thrust, all I could think of was, "This will bring me one step closer to holding my son."

Thank God he finished quickly and we drove back to his lawyer's office. Problem solved. I thanked his attorney for his understanding and announced we were heading north to re-establish our family.

My father-in-law was not a happy man. More importantly, Mr. Franklin was astonished; he had been searching all over for me. His face literally became devoid of color. He had been working endlessly with Judge H. to resolve this matter. Those were too many failed attempts for me. I was finished waiting. I had taken matters into my own hands.

Gavin, Mr. Franklin, and I drove the rental car back to my in-laws' shack and I was reunited with my son. I could feel life return to my body. I still hadn't eaten, but I was re-energized being with Devin and feeling one step closer to victory. Victory in full meant being in my hometown with my son.

Devin was filthy dirty. He was completely unkempt and

walking around in a diaper that appeared to be from the night before. He was disgusting. The look on my mother-in-law's face when I walked in to her home was priceless. To add insult to her injury, I scooped up my dirty son, brought him into her bathroom, locked the door, and took a thirty-minute bath with my little boy. As I sat in the tub cleaning the dirt from my son and the lingering odor of intercourse with a man I truly loathed, I felt more power and more control in that very moment than ever before in my life. It was a baptism for Devin and me, our new beginning. We were starting out clean and fresh. I was in control of this situation and f*** them all.

After the bath, we dressed while Gavin packed and headed out the door. Mr. Franklin made all the travel arrangements and we drove off for the airport. As we were walking to the car, I will never forget my mother-in-law saying to me in a low tone not intended to be heard by others, "If anything happens to my son, you will answer to me."

I responded in the same low and bitter tone, "F*** you." I smiled sweetly and got into the car.

I ate en route to the airport. It was my first meal in five days. I couldn't get much into my stomach, but I did eat. By the time I got on a scale at home, I had lost nine pounds.

We arrived back at our apartment early Thursday morning. It seemed like a lifetime had passed since that previous Friday night. I slept a few hours with Devin at my side. I awoke and continued my "happy wife" role as I dressed my son and told Gavin we were going shopping. I brought Devin to a safe location. My attorney had already notified Judge H. that we had arrived safely home. Mr. Franklin was still unaware that I was playing a role. I was an actress. After bringing Devin to my safe location, I spoke with my attorney and advised him that I had

Devin and I wanted full custody. There was a strange, silent pause on the phone.

Apparently, Mr. Franklin had informed my attorney and the judge that I was staying married. He had believed everything that he had seen and had believed it was my intention to reconcile. There had been no opportunity in the past day to let Mr. Franklin know otherwise. He let me know that I was quite convincing. I had to explain that if I didn't take matters into my own hands, this situation might not have ended in my favor. I knew that the legal system was not working efficiently despite everyone's best efforts.

Mr. Franklin, Judge H and my lawyer couldn't believe what I had accomplished. A court hearing was scheduled about the same time I returned to my apartment to speak with Gavin. I was alone and the conversation was brief. I remember saying, "I'll see you in court" as I prepared to walk out on my old life forever. He stood there in shock and stared at me in disbelief. I left in haste, fearful that he might turn violent.

A year-long custody battle began when I left the apartment that day. In the end, Gavin lost custody of Devin. The same day the judge ruled in my favor, Gavin moved back to his hometown and essentially abandoned his son. He has seen Devin approximately six times in the past 30 years. I recently learned that Gavin's father passed away. The last words he spoke to me were, "You're as good as dead in your son's eyes, so why don't you just move on?"

I remember it like it was yesterday. Thirty years passed and I never received a call or card to apologize for his tremendously hurtful actions or words. He never saw his grandson again and lived till his dying day blaming me.

CHAPTER 6

Learning to Heal

I have no regrets about my choice to be a single mother. I rented a two-bedroom apartment and moved us into our new world, our new beginning. Gavin continued to create any roadblocks in his power to make this transition painful. Rather than engage with him in ridiculous battles over belongings, I decided to leave with just the essentials. I took my son and our beds. I left all the other furniture behind. Couches, tables, dishes remained with Gavin in my old world. They represented my past. I didn't need them or want them. Gavin did. So, he could have it all. He was welcome to all the furniture and the memories that remained. I wanted new beginnings. I had no desire and no energy to fight for objects that were replaceable.

My priority was happiness. For the first time in my life, I felt that I was in control of my destiny. It seemed that my Light was beginning to faintly glow once again. I had a big new apartment and no furniture to put in it. But I was happy. I recall the feeling of overwhelming joy as I set out to make a new life for Devin and myself. I can do this. I can make this work, I told myself. Let the journey begin.

Being a mom was my most important job. To spend as much time with Devin as possible, I did what many nurses choose to do: I continued to work the night shift so I could earn money

33

while my son slept. Then, I would be home during the daytime hours when he was awake. It was very important to me to spend days with my son. For me, working nights was great for two reasons. First, it alleviated the guilt of having to go to work and leave my son behind. If I was working while Devin was sleeping, I didn't feel like I was missing a huge piece of his development. Second, the night shift paid more per hour, so I could work fewer hours weekly to make ends meet. Therefore, I was able to be home more with Devin.

This time in my life was a financial struggle. Despite court intervention, which obligated Gavin to pay child support for his son, I rarely saw any money from him. A few months after we separated, the court awarded me full custody of Devin and with that decision, Gavin moved away. He emptied our old apartment and returned to his hometown, nearly a thousand miles from his son. He advised the court that this move was only temporary, but nearly 30 years have passed and he has barely set foot in this county since. It was nearly impossible to enforce a child support order from that distance. I lived check by check and had little opportunity to save for the future, but that was okay because I was free from a destructive relationship.

Even though I didn't have any furniture, I did have a television and a VCR. Devin and I would sit on the floor with large throw pillows and watch Disney videos together. It was a simple life, but simple was very sweet at that time.

I could not have survived during that time without the continued love and support of family. My father or sister would sleep over to be with Devin on the nights I worked. I was fortunate that I didn't have to budget the additional costs of childcare on my salary, still trying to manage to pay off the exorbitant legal fees. Devin always had loving family members to watch over him and to support our transition from nuclear family to a single-parent family with lots of loving support. Most important, we were still a family.

Despite the distance between Gavin and I, there was the Shadow of daily fear that my son would be abducted again. I had nightmares where Devin was missing. I would call for him and my calls would become more panic-filled with each moment that Devin did not respond. I would awaken in fear and run into Devin's bedroom to find him asleep and safe. Each day of my new life challenged me with anxiety and fear that if I took my eyes off my son for a split second, he would be gone.

Surviving a child's abduction changes the family dynamic forever. I was consciously aware that I had just regained custody of my son through my own deception of leading Gavin to believe that we were going to remain married. Then, I was granted custody through the legal process. Yet the legal process did not give me any false hope of security. I understood clearly the limitations of the legal system and could not fully rely on it to protect my son if he was abducted again. It was a terribly frightening time for me.

Gavin was emotionally unstable. He had proven this by his previous actions. I had no reason to believe that he had regret for the pain he caused; rather he only had regret for believing in my sincerity that I wanted to continue our relationship and returning to our home. He was even more angry and bitter than he had been when he abducted Devin. I understood this.

Each day of Devin's young life, I remained in a simmering state of fear, knowing that attempts to re-abduct my son were possible. I knew this fear was valid. It was because of this fear that Devin became the victim of a more protective and sheltered life than most kids. By the time he was old enough for school, the principal and teachers would have complete legal documents on file to protect Devin from any preventable events.

We teach our children at a young age not to talk to strangers and how to defend themselves against predators. Unfortunately for Devin, he had to learn that he needed to be cautious if his father or relatives of his father approached him. I felt like my son lost a large part of his innocence because he had to learn that family might be unsafe too.

Yet to the outside world, I wore my mask of "normal," the mask that told people that I fit in and my life was no different from theirs. The mask I had worn from my earliest memories confirmed for me that my life was different, that my life was wrong. What I didn't realize till recently was that I was teaching my son the same trick. Put on your mask, son. No one will be able to see your life is different. Only you and I will know.

CHAPTER 7

Fatal Attraction

Looking out the window of my apartment one summer morning the following year, I noticed my upstairs neighbor leaving for work. My sister was visiting and we peeked through the blinds like a couple of high school girls watching him leave. We giggled and whispered about him and put imaginary bets on whether or not he was gay or straight.

We learned his name was Steve and that he lived with another guy in the apartment directly above mine. He was very handsome with dark hair and dark eyes, but his ethnicity wasn't obvious to us. Our guess was he had a Spanish background or some other Hispanic blend. He didn't seem to fit into my rural community, but neither did I. I had lived in the apartment beneath him for a year yet, we never really crossed paths. I was going to change that.

One morning I watched out the front window, waiting for him to return home. I had a plan. I was going to open my front door to leave at the same time he was opening his front door to return. Brilliant! Masterful!

I was glad I thought of it. I had no clue what would happen next.

"Oh excuse, me," I said shyly.

"No problem," he replied.

I fumbled for something in my handbag and appeared out of sorts. "Do you need some help?" he asked like a gentleman. One thing led to the next and within days we were on our first date. Note to my sister: He is not gay.

Our first date was a movie at the local cinema. We had a good time and by the end of the night I was hooked, I mean completely blind-sided by what I believed was love. I had never felt that way before and I could not imagine my life without him.

We spent about the next year together. Unfortunately it didn't take that long to determine we weren't meant to last. Somewhere in that year, talking became arguing. Steve was in his twenties like me and focused on building his career, not on settling down. I was dreaming about being a wife again and having another baby someday.

We broke up, we got back together and we broke up again. It was another roller coaster relationship, ups and downs, but each time one of us got off the ride for some reason, we got back on. Eventually, we did separate completely. But, what neither of us expected hit us like a ton of bricks on my 26th birthday.

Still working the night shift, I turned 26 years old after midnight. My sister and a couple of close girlfriends I worked with were heading to a nearby bar to celebrate my birthday that evening. It was all planned. We were going to have a fabulous time full of potential to meet Mr. Wonderful. But, I didn't feel well that night. I was a bit nauseous and more tired than I should be, so I took advantage of one of my perks as a nurse, and sent my urine to the hospital lab for a pregnancy test. Surprise and Happy Birthday!! I was pregnant.

I was floored to say the least. Steve and I had broken up for good more than three weeks before. We just could not communicate. Now what? Happy Birthday to me! Twenty-six years old, single, still legally married and baby number two was on the way. WTF!

In my shock and disbelief, I decided to page Steve and make arrangements to discuss the news. It was about 2 a.m., but I knew he would be awake. He returned my call and was a bit more irritable than I had hoped for. I asked him if we could get together to talk, but he declined. I explained that it was pretty important, but he was already in a foul mood for whatever reason, so rather than beg for time I just blurted out my news, "I'm pregnant."

Silence…more silence…

Finally, after several minutes passed I said, "Are you there?"

He replied, in a painfully bitter tone, "What are you going to do about it?"

Quietly and honestly I responded, "I don't know." His last words to me at that time were, "Well, if you decide to keep it, you are on your own."

With that, he hung up the phone. I didn't hear from him again for more than a month.

Although we were not a couple, my hopeless romantic self wanted to believe that Steve would see the Light. He would recognize we were meant to be together, it would all work out. Remembering these times, I feel sad for the naïve me that believed in fairy tales and romance. I believed I could make him want me. I could become what he was looking for. It took years for me to see the true person he was and frightfully similar to my narcissistic mother. This unplanned pregnancy was not going to derail Steve's ambition and I was not going to end it for fear of being alone. Somehow God was going to help me get through this challenge.

The month with no communication from Steve was a difficult one. But, after much prayer and internal struggle I decided

I was keeping the baby. I had no intention to cause Steve any pain and I had no intention to trap him in a loveless relationship. I did intend to keep this child and do the best I could in the situation.

My mother learned about my pregnancy through the family gossip chain soon after I made my choice to keep the baby. I did not receive a call of congratulations or support in my decision, rather I heard third-hand that my mother's response was, "She's not keeping it is she?"

So, the lack of motherly support in my life continued. I was facing a new challenge and trying to do the best I could in this situation. Once again, I was on my own. Soon there would be another soul joining my world of dysfunction.

Internally, I heard a voice over and over again telling me it was shameful to have two children by two different fathers, especially, since Gavin and I were still legally married. I felt embarrassed and ashamed that I was carrying a second child by a father who would not give me the time of day. But, I tried my best to maintain a positive view. I had a good career and I was going to be a mother again. One thing I did resign myself to was that I was going to be a single woman for quite a long time. In this situation, with two kids by different fathers, I would not be able to buy a date.

I wish I could say that I left Steve proudly and stood on my own two feet. But, the devastation of being alone in combination with the pregnancy hormones really turned me into a desperate and pathetic person. On more than one occasion, I reduced myself to begging him on my knees not to abandon me and to please be supportive. I recall like it was yesterday the emptiness in his eyes when for the last time he shut his apartment door and ignored my cries. I spent the remainder of my pregnancy in shame as I learned that he was dating someone else while I was carrying his child.

When I learned that Steve was dating again, despite our situation, I realized just how disposable my unborn child and I were to him. Steve had moved on, but I was stuck.

Equally painful was the knowledge that another woman would actually become involved with a man who was so viciously unsupportive of his pregnant ex-girlfriend. I think that was even harder for me to process at the time. To me, women are supposed to uplift and support each other. It is some kind of unwritten code. I couldn't understand how another woman would want to be with a man who was openly and consciously rejecting another woman who was in a vulnerable position that he helped create.

However, through this experience I began to see with more clear vision just how cutthroat women can be to each other. All women do not share the unwritten code I believe in. This would not be the first time I learned this difficult lesson. I think that this experience may have unconsciously contributed to my desire to attend to women as a midwife, to uplift and support them, rather than tear down or weaken.

In order to prepare for my additional upcoming expenses, I moved into a smaller, more affordable apartment. I had no financial help, so I needed to exercise as much caution as possible to remain solvent. It was probably also better to remain physically distanced from Steve.

Devin and I settled into our new apartment well and watched my belly grow with each passing day. Devin was excited he was going to be a big brother and we would speak daily about his responsibility to love and protect his brother or sister. Our new arrival was expected right around Devin's 5th birthday.

Obviously, Steve and I would have failed miserably if we chose to stay together. This pregnancy was not one of love, support and joy but it was mine and I embraced my unborn child with anticipation and desire to be a good mother. My circumstances were far from ideal and brought with it shame for me that I had gotten into this situation. But all of this was tempered by the joy of being a mother again. With each new day with this anticipation, I wore my mask of "normal" and pretended all was well.

I held on to a fantastic notion that one day Steve would change his mind and recognize the error of his ways. I prayed that he would contact me and profess his love for me and his desire to be a family. Eventually, he did, but by then it was far too late.

CHAPTER 8

Mystical Guidance

I have had an interest in the mystical including Channels, Mediums and Intuitives for as long as I can remember. It has been part of my soul's longing to connect with the God Source, more intimately. The belief in Guardian Angels, Spirits, Dark Energies has always aligned with my Spirit and although raised Roman Catholic, much of the doctrine of that religion and others simply does not align. I bring no judgement with these words and have absolute respect for personal choice in more than just spiritual beliefs. I am a trained nurse practitioner with an earned doctorate in public health from prestigious academic institutions. I hold in high regard the importance of balance between science and art when it comes to maintaining health and preventing illness. I have also gone on record as admitting my belief in the ongoing duality of Light vs Darkness that humanity is experiencing.

To many I am an enigma. A self-identifying Starseed that spent decades striving to overcome her personal demons by choosing healing as a profession. I am a nurse. I am a midwife. Honored to be both. I believe in the gifts of mystics including the more famous names like Edgar Cayce. Over the years, I have seen more than one tarot card reader and intuitive. During my second pregnancy I frequented two. Both were great ladies and I appreciated the kindness and sensitivity they gave me as I sought direction and hope for my future. I was not concerned about my mission and purpose during this challenging time, I was simply seeking confirmation that Steve would change his mind and we would be a happy family. I remained hopeful that if I gave him the space he needed to process this life's change, he would have his own epiphany.

The clairvoyants did not confirm that my earnest wishes would come true. The prediction was I would date and possibly marry a man named Larry. They also predicted that as I moved on with my life and was no longer interested in Steve, he would return and want to reunite with me. They added that there would be someone named Larry and that I already knew him.

I wracked my brain trying to figure out the identity of this Larry person whom I might one day marry. I drew a blank.

Steve was not going to be the one, the readers said. By that time, I was six months pregnant and desperate for hope that Steve would return and my intolerable situation would improve.

I meditated on these predictions and continued with my daily rituals in anticipation of change in the near future. I waited for Larry to reveal himself to me, believing from that moment forward that Larry's emergence would be the best chance that Steve would want to reunite with me.

When I returned home from my readings, I shared the news of my predicted future with my sister. Both of my psychic counselors allowed their sessions to be taped, so I could play the tapes and my sister and I would do our own self-assessment of the messages. We maintained watchful waiting, but I swore I did not know any man named Larry.

One day at the nearby grocery store, I was picking up a few things for dinner. I was well into my eighth month of pregnancy. I was large and quite awkward as I waddled through the aisles. As

I approached the checkout line I heard a familiar voice greeting me, "Hey Stace, how are you doing?"

I turned to my right and in the next checkout aisle was a guy that I had seen at the gym before I stopped working out due to my advancing pregnancy.

"Oh. Hi, Larry," I responded and answered that everything in life was status quo.

Larry lacked subtlety (he still does) as he gave me the full body scan that largely focused on my growing belly. "Wow, you are big!" he noted, giving voice to the obvious. This was the best response he could come up with at the moment?

I smiled politely, thinking sarcastically, "Brilliant! Very well put."

But I understood there was no malicious intent. Larry was a very nice guy. So, I remained pleasant and told him that I was nearing the end of my pregnancy.

We spoke for several minutes while we waited in line and we were quite surprised to learn that we both were living in the same apartment complex. He was living on one end and had moved in recently. I was living on the opposite end and had also just moved in. Before leaving the store, Larry asked me my apartment number and wished me the best of luck with the upcoming delivery.

Not once did I connect the psychics' readings with this chance meeting. I felt no physical attraction to him and I would expect him to have no physical attraction toward me in my current state. Not unless he had a screw loose, of course.

Within a week of running into Larry at the grocery store, I returned home to find a gift bag hanging on the doorknob. The gift inside was neatly wrapped. As I entered my apartment and placed my belongings on the table I wondered who would leave me a gift. I opened it carefully. It was a book. *The Emotionally Abused Woman* written by Beverly Engel with no card attached. Who would leave this book for me and why? My sister showed up and, putting on her detective cap, was determined to solve the mystery. She began to flip the pages in the book and the sender became apparent. The sender had written the most thoughtful and considerate message inside the front cover. It was Larry.

Larry! The puzzle pieces began to fall into place in my mind.

"He likes you," my sister smirked.

"Don't be an idiot!" I snapped back defending his honor, "He is just trying to be a nice guy." I called him to thank him for his kindness. I told him that I appreciated his thoughtfulness and would let him know when the baby arrived.

Within a few weeks, my second son arrived and we recovered quietly in the home I tried to create for the innocent souls that chose me as their mother. Our first moments together remain etched in my mind as with each of my children. Pure joy, pure love, purity in humanity that is only experienced during the miracle of childbirth. I wasn't sure I could love another as much as I did my first son, but that notion becomes instantly illogical with each child. This new soul was part of my family; good, bad, and ugly. I promised to put my best foot forward and provide a life better than I had, with or without a father.

Steve did attend the delivery and then left me to recover and raise my children alone just like he had vowed months earlier. I should have been scared to death, but I had faith. I was a single mom. I had a great job. I was going to hold my head up and smile and do my best. Failure wasn't an option. After returning from the hospital, I made a few phone calls. I called Larry, who congratulated me and we discussed a few details about the birth experience. A few minutes into the conversation, Larry invited me to join him and a few friends to a football game in a few weeks. I thanked him for the offer, but wasn't sure if I could accept with a brand-new baby. I told him I would have to get back to him before I could commit.

"I told you he likes you!" flew out of my sister's mouth before I barely hung up the phone. She then offered to watch my children, so that I could go to a football game, get out of my apartment and have a little bit of fun.

My sister encouraged me to make plans. "You need to get out and have some fun, Stacey, just go."

It felt wrong to go out and leave my new baby. I remember feeling like I didn't deserve to have fun. I was a mother and my children needed me. They didn't need a babysitter while I took off to a football game and left them behind. My sister wholeheartedly disagreed and fervently encouraged me to call Larry and accept his invitation.

So I did.

It was autumn, and I was off to my first football game. It was an absolutely gorgeous fall day, one that I hope to never forget. Larry picked me up and we met the other couples at the game. I had a great time despite the feeling that all eyes were on me. The single woman who just had a baby two weeks ago, wearing her mask, pretending to be normal while trying intently to cover the shame she wore on the inside. I was self-conscious, but I worked through my insecurities and remained pleasant hoping for a good day.

By the end of the game, I was very happy that Larry had asked me to join them. We returned to my apartment and he met Dax for the first time. He even asked to if he could hold the baby. Larry held this tiny newborn baby with natural gentleness. I appreciated his kindness and thanked God for the new friend.

CHAPTER 9

My Next Chapter

Larry and I began to see each other more frequently after that first football "not a date" in October. We began to go to dinner on weekends and talk on the phone several times a week. We weren't dating in any official capacity. I liked him. I just didn't like him in that way. You understand, the sexual way.

I was still recovering from Dax's birth, so taking sexual interest in any man was not on my list of important things to do. But I definitely enjoyed Larry's company. He had a natural way of taking my mind off of my everyday stressors and just bringing me simple happy times again. I appreciated that.

Larry will tell you that he was not the physical type that I was generally drawn too. He pointed out to me that I was naturally drawn to dark-haired, dark-eyed men. I had never paid attention before, but he certainly saw in me a pattern and he was right on the mark. Larry is light-haired and light-eyed with a significantly thinning hairline. I suppose in hindsight the fact that he was losing his hair in his thirties was something that was not attractive to me at that time. But, I enjoyed his company and we continued to be friends.

I recall during this same time, Lynn, my girlfriend's mother, tried to fix me up on a blind date with a guy named Al. She sang praises for this guy she worked with and thought he was, "just my type." I had never been on a blind date before, but my girlfriend talked me into it.

I met this guy for dinner. He was a sheriff in our local jail. All I can say is first impressions truly do speak volumes. He was very tall. I suppose near six feet five inches or more with light brown hair and a few teeth missing when he smiled.

"Ugh!" I thought. "I am going to kill Mary when I see her."

I remained pleasant through the meal and declined dessert. I felt so bad for Al and his hard luck story about paying alimony for four children that I gladly bought my own meal. I just wanted to get out of there.

Throughout my ride home, I kept thinking of Larry and wondering what he was doing. This was the first time I realized just how much I missed him when he was not around. Rather than heading straight home, I went to Larry's apartment first and gathered up my nerve to knock on his door.

We weren't dating so I felt awkward knowing that he might be with someone else. He was alone. He answered the door and asked me how the date went. We both laughed as I shared my first and last blind date experience. Then, I did it. I told him how much I missed him and how I thought of him throughout the entire meal. He looked at me, smiled (with a full complement of teeth), and in that moment, he kissed me. It was really nice.

It was close to three months of dating/not-dating and still no sex. I was not ready to make that commitment again, especially with the baggage of my background. I just could not bring myself to risk being hurt again. I liked Larry. I liked him even more than I had anticipated, but sex brings a relationship to a whole different level. I just did not feel prepared for that.

He never pressured me. Not once. We enjoyed each other's

company and somehow evolved into not dating other people, but sex wasn't happening . . . yet.

People who watched television in the early 90s will recall that *90210* and *Melrose Place* used to air consecutively once a week. My sister and I never missed the episodes and even had our own ritual of talking to each other on the phone for nearly the entire two hours. During one of these mini-drama nights, my sister and I started a discussion about sex and she reminded me that it had been several months since I had any. We were laughing and carrying on and being sisterly stupid when she starting suggesting to me that I should go knock on Larry's door and "do it." We laughed at the thought of it, but I rejected the idea and told her it wasn't happening. My sister remained persistent and asked me what I had to lose.

"Go ahead and just do it. It's been a long time," she continued.

So I started thinking and finally agreed to go for it. Really, what did I have to lose? Well, I answered myself, I could lose my self- respect. Again.

In our master plan, we agreed that my sister would come over to my apartment to babysit and I would go to Larry's apartment during commercial break with the intention of "doing it."

Commercials started when my sister arrived. She wished me luck and I was out the door. I only had about six minutes before the show began again, so I was in a hurry.

Knock, knock, knock.

"Hey, what are you doing here?" he asked as he answered his door. "No time for small talk," I thought to myself as I kissed him, no more words necessary. He got the hint.

Jackpot! We did it.

"No time to discuss now, the commercials are over, got to run. Bye."

51

With that, I was out the door and back to my apartment. I looked at my sister with a big cheesy smile.

"Did you do it?" she asked. I just nodded and no more was said.

Larry and I continued to date and in less than six months, I was hooked. It was one of the snowiest winters in our area in many years and Larry and I were together most of his free time. We would speak on the phone each day. Several nights a week he would join us for dinner. Weekends were together. I began to miss him when we weren't together. Larry became the man in my children's life. He was the one that fed solid food to my little one first. He took them to the playground. He watched them so I could nap. With no children of his own and no expectations he came into my world and brought sunshine back into my family's world. Soon our time spent watching the snow fall turned into planning our future together.

It was truly a magical season for me, a season filled with very special memories. My children were thriving, my personal life was changing for the better and I was no longer crying every day. I was smiling.

Steve had been absent from the time of my second son's birth and it just didn't matter. Actually, at that moment, I was relieved he wasn't around. My life was once again in a place of healing.

One snowy night, Larry and I had returned from a fabulous dinner and it seemed we connected in a deeper way. That night our relationship transformed from simple sex to making love. I went into the living room to put on the Late Show and as I looked back toward the bedroom I caught a brief glimpse of Larry as he walked naked toward the bathroom. He was very fit and for the first time, I saw him in a more intimate and loving way. I remember thinking at that very moment, "I could get used to this."

Fast forward 25 years: I still feel the same way.

If you ask either one of us who proposed, we don't know. We really don't recall how our dating transitioned to an engagement, but it did and one day we were planning our wedding. I do remember being adamant that I could not live with him without being engaged. I was not comfortable bringing my children into a live-in environment with another man if I wasn't getting married. Larry respected that and we did eventually move in together as our wedding preparations were under way. At the time, we hadn't exactly decided on an engagement ring, but our wedding plans had begun. After we made love to christen our very first night together in our new living space we snuggled up together and began to speak about what the next day was going to bring.

As we started to outline our future, Larry took my left hand and placed the most gorgeous diamond engagement ring on my finger. It was exactly the one I wanted. It was the very ring I showed to my mother one rare day when we were shopping at the mall. Her devastating response: "What makes you think you deserve something like that?" cut through my very soul.

Thankfully, Larry thought I deserved it as he smiled and gently told me that he didn't want me to spend one night living with him without being officially engaged. He made sure I was wearing an engagement ring before I went to sleep in our bed for the first time. My future husband, the romantic.

Our wedding was set for autumn the following year. Larry and I worked within a budget and plans were going well. I only had one minor detail to correct by then: I needed a divorce.

Years had passed and Gavin still refused my repeated requests for a divorce. Gavin knew nothing about my second pregnancy, my wedding plans or anything about his son. He just refused to divorce me. We had no assets, so it wasn't about money. I had left the majority of the furniture and our belongings with him the day I moved out. Gavin simply refused to let me go.

My attorney had a big undertaking ahead of him to secure my divorce in the seven months before the wedding. Larry was very concerned, but I kept telling him not to worry about it. Of course, he didn't completely believe me.

A court date was finally set in the state Supreme Court in August, just one month before my wedding to Larry. I kept my fingers crossed despite the fact that my attorney had warned me it might still take several months for the judge to sign divorce papers even after the trial. I carried on in faith that everything would be okay.

In the meantime, my attorney attempted several times to settle the divorce stipulations before the actual trial date, but Gavin wouldn't budge. As the process unfolded, it was determined that Gavin was in arrears close to $15,000 in child support for Devin. He had not paid anything for the years we had been apart and when the dollars were tallied he was in debt to me for a large sum of money. In order to secure my divorce, Gavin wanted me to waive that dollar amount in exchange for his promise that he would not contest our divorce any further.

I thought about it. I discussed it with Larry. My final decision was to agree to Gavin's extortion. I had to face the fact that Gavin was a deadbeat dad and I took some small comfort knowing that he had to go to sleep at night knowing that. I had been providing for my son all these years and never had any belief that I was going to actually see that money anyway. So, I agreed and went before the judge in September to finalize my divorce. The proceeding was uneventful until the very end when my attorney spoke to the judge.

"Oh, one more thing, Your Honor," he said, "My client has a wedding planned in one month, so we respectfully request that Your Honor sign these papers as expeditiously as possible."

The judge's eyebrows raised and his face contorted just a little bit as he responded, "I'll see what I can do."

The divorce papers were in my hand ten days before my wedding. I did it!

It is important for me to share another event on the day of my wedding. I was lying in the bathtub, trying my best to stay relaxed as I prepared for the amazing night that was ahead. The children and Larry were not home and I had created a peaceful space for the few hours that led up to the more chaotic wedding preparations with hair, makeup, dress, etc. This was really the first quiet moment I had in months. As I lay in the soothing warm tub planning the rest of my day, the telephone rang.

"Hello?" I asked as I sank into the bubbles.

"Stacey?"

I recognized the voice on the other end instantly. My heart immediately sank. It was Steve.

"What do you want?" I asked reluctantly anticipating trouble knowing that he was calling on that specific day.

"I don't want you to get married," he said very quietly, almost in an adolescent voice.

"I think you need to re-think it and not get married," he added. "I've been thinking about it and I think we should talk about being a family."

He paused and waited for my response. My head was spinning. I couldn't believe these words were really being spoken.

I was silent for quite a while before I finally replied, "I am getting married in less than six hours."

In this brief moment of contemplation that seemed like an eternity, everything that I thought I once desired was being offered to me. The psychics were right: I was faced with the decision that I cried and prayed for endlessly during my pregnancy with Dax.

"Good bye Steve," I softly said as I hung up the phone and cried in my bathwater. How dare he? I thought. Why now?

Larry and I were married that evening. It was nearly one year after the football game. As we stood before God, family and friends and recited our vows, Larry promised to love me and my children. I still don't fully understand why he would take on this burden, but more concerning to me was whether or not I was going to be able to keep my secret from him. I am not normal. My life is not normal. I wear a mask of normal, but I was fearful what would happen if he found out it was all a façade. I was grateful for his love, but spent my days fearful of when he would learn of my horrible truth. What would be of this marriage when he realized I was broken? That I was not worthy of love and not capable of being normal?

CHAPTER 10

New Chapter,
New Challenges

The adjustment to married life was not without its challenges. In addition to being a new wife and mother to two young children, I had returned to college with the goal of advancing my nursing degree. I wanted to be a midwife, but for that, I needed more education and experience. I had never given up my childhood dream of supporting women and empowering them in the birth process. When I was a little girl, I was the labor coach for my pet tabby cat as she delivered her kittens. I wanted to learn how to deliver human babies.

This goal was a six-year path of additional college to finish my undergraduate and graduate studies. Before Larry and I were engaged, I had already made the decision to return to school. He remained supportive of me and stood behind me every step of the way.

Yet, this was a tough time. Each of us was adjusting to being part of a new family unit. Devin was six and the baby was a year old when I married Larry. We bought our first home and controlled chaos began. We were all adjusting, but life felt good.

As the boys were growing out of diapers and becoming little people, I began yearning for another baby. I can recall a deep aching with every ovulatory cycle to have another child. I would resist the urge for several months at a time, then the urge would take over and I would ask Larry for another baby. He would try to nicely let me down while providing all the practical reasons why it wasn't a good idea. Two children are enough, you are still in college, I don't feel the need to have a child of my own. But, I persisted.

It wasn't like I was trying to purposefully create more turmoil in our busy world. I could absolutely agree with all logical reasons presented, but there is an often-underappreciated power within our human bodies identified as hormones. Sexuality in all species is influenced by the endocrine system/hormones. For me, the desire to have a third child was so strong it was as if I was being manipulated mid-cycle of each menstruation. I didn't only want a baby. I felt like I needed a baby. This was quite different then my last two pregnancies when I wasn't expecting or desiring to be pregnant. So, it was a warm summer day, approximately years into our marriage, when I recall approaching Larry when he was outside doing yard work

"Do you think we could have another baby, PLEASE?" I asked with a grin on my face that I suppose Larry could interpret as either joking or serious.

"What?" he asked as he continued to whack weeds along the perimeter of the house.

I repeated the question.

"I don't want to talk about this now," he answered, ending the conversation for the moment, but I knew he would come back to it for me.

Later that evening, Larry reiterated the already well known and quite legitimate reasons why having another baby was not a good idea. Money, time and hard work were included. I rebutted with my innate hormonal drive that was motivating me and although he was never hurtful, he wouldn't concede. The subject ended, but only temporarily.

Over the next few years, I periodically returned to my desire to have another baby. It seemed I just couldn't give up. I really wanted another baby. By this time, I was in the home stretch of my college studies. I was in my early thirties and feeling internal pressure that if I didn't have a baby soon, I would likely lose the opportunity to my biological clock. So, I persisted with Larry and brought up my same argument again.

"Please," this time as the tears rolled down my face. "Just one more baby?"

He remained firm with his one syllable answer, "No!"

I walked away, defeated again.

Then out of nowhere, after four years of trying unsuccessfully to persuade Larry, we were sitting in a local restaurant on a Saturday night I said jokingly to him, "You know I am ovulating?"

With that, I truly expected some form of a sarcastic response intended to change the subject without hurting my feelings once again. Larry just sat there eating his meal. It seemed like several minutes passed before he spoke. Then he looked up at me and smiled and said, "Okay."

Dinner ended without dessert as I hastily asked for the check. This was the first time he had agreed to try to make a baby and I wanted to get him home to bed before he changed his mind.

I will never forget that night. We made a true attempt to start our new life together while Marvin Gaye played *Let's Get it On* in the background. For me, as much as I adore my two children, it was my first time to create a life willingly. That evening was one of the most special evenings I have shared with my husband.

When we had finished, in the typical Larry fashion that I cherish each day, he got out of bed and said, "That ought to do it!" as he proceeded to the bathroom.

I smiled and lay still hopeful that he was right and in a few weeks we would share some very special news. I had never tried to get pregnant before, so this moment for me was part of my healing from the dysfunction that had long been part of my life. It symbolized a transition to my new life of "normal." I had worked for it.

Larry loved me enough to be a wonderful father to his stepchildren and finally he had agreed to bring forth a new life with me. I was bathed in love that I had never experienced before. I was being given the opportunity to be pregnant in the more traditional sense. A pregnancy planned in a nuclear family. An opportunity to heal the deep shame (Shadow) I had been suppressing for years. Not only the shame of being an unwed mother, but the shame of not being wanted by my parents. Within this Shadow, deep scars that were unspoken and not consciously understood by me. The depth of pain had yet to reveal, but to me this pregnancy represented proof that a man could love me. I was lovable.

Several months passed with no new pregnancy, fueling my suspicions that something wasn't right. I was nearing graduation as a nurse midwife and could diagnose there was an issue not certain what the issue was. I was worried that there was something wrong with me, so I sought counsel with my gynecologist. Success finally came with the assistance of medication that increased my egg production and more targeted intercourse that was monitored through blood work to determine the precise day of ovulation. I received scheduled injections that either suppressed or enhanced ovulation for a few months.

By April Larry and I learned we were pregnant—with twins! The pregnancy was confirmed by ultrasound and we were in shock, but not unpleasantly so. We returned home to tell the children our family was growing. I was ecstatic!

The pregnancy was going well and we were both adjusting to the notion of two babies coming home. We were having the practical conversations about cribs, strollers and making decisions about buying a minivan.

I was not happy with the idea of a minivan. I did not consider myself the "minivan mom" type and I really was looking for a better solution. By week 15 of my pregnancy, I was off to the doctors for my ultrasound and check-up. I couldn't wait to see a picture of my growing babies and hear the updates. In a million years, I never anticipated I would receive such horrible news.

It appeared that one of the twins was extremely and significantly deformed. The deformities did not follow any specific genetic condition like Down's syndrome, but the doctor gently informed me the defects were "incompatible with life."

In other words, the baby might survive inside my body, but it would certainly not survive outside. My head spun as I digested the words. I felt like the life was being sucked out of my body as I tried to comprehend that I was going to lose the baby that I had not yet met.

"Isn't there something we can do?" I pleaded for answers and repeatedly suggested a mistake must have been made, even though in my heart I knew no mistake was made. My doctors are very experienced and they were much more knowledgeable than I was. My baby, our baby, was not well and decisions needed to be made quickly.

These decisions involved protecting our other unborn baby. He seemed quite perfect, but the doctors warned us that there were risks to his wellbeing as a result of being in the same environment with his unhealthy twin.

Larry and I were bombarded with discussions and options about pre-term labor and genetic diseases. One thing I did know was that there was no way a child of mine was going to become a hospital experiment. If my child's deformities were truly incompatible with life, then I wasn't going to risk him living for even a few moments and becoming a scientific experiment that ultimately would delay his inevitable death.

Working in medicine exposes health care workers to a more complete understanding of the tragedy that often comes with dying in a medical facility. Dying in a hospital involves machines and intravenous tubes with fluids and blood being drawn intermittently.

An ill newborn is not going to be allowed to die peacefully. Instead, there may be a grueling and painful attempt to preserve and prolong the inevitable. I personally couldn't bear to see it happen if I knew for sure that my child truly had a terminal condition. That being understood, we had only two options.

Option 1: Do nothing. Let the pregnancy and the circumstances play out as they would.

Option 2: A doctor in Manhattan had recently developed a technique that was designed for reducing multiple pregnancies down to a more manageable size. Basically, women who were pregnant with several fetuses could opt to reduce down to maybe a triplet or twin size. The technique was quite new, but was promising hope for women in tragic situations like ours.

Larry and I made an appointment to talk with this physician. We didn't know what to expect, but we needed to learn more about this procedure.

Dr. B called it "selective reduction," a specialized procedure that can bring a multiple pregnancy down to a safer gestational size. It was very new at the time I was pregnant and had only been done a handful of times. With the circumstances we faced, we needed to be absolutely sure that our child did indeed have the significant anomalies that were being described. So, we wanted absolute confirmation that our baby was not going to live outside of my womb and would likely die soon and threaten his healthy twin.

After careful discussion of our expectations and multiple tests completed by Dr. B, he confirmed the worst. With much prayer and so many tears, Larry and I agreed this might be our only chance to protect both babies. We saw no other option that suited our spiritual and personal values, so we proceeded to the next step with complete faith in Dr. B.

The whole experience was terrible. This many years later, as I write about it, the tears come to my eyes and my heart aches. We never discussed with our families the details of what we experienced and the choices we faced.

To this day, they are unaware of the specifics of our personal challenge that strengthened us as a couple, but could have easily broken us. We endured a heart-wrenching death of a child we were unable to hold, but were able to see by ultrasound. Time and time again, we saw the birth defects that were pointed out to us before we made our decision. We loved our baby just as if he was as perfect as the first snow of winter. We loved him, we wanted him, but more than that we couldn't bear thinking of him suffering even if only for a few moments. This soul was not meant to join us. Spared of the dysfunction or joining us briefly to impart wisdom and guidance for what our future would bring?

We saw his brother, who appeared to be healthy and thriving and we loved him just as much. We grieved the loss of one son as we celebrated the growth of another. It was a bittersweet day filled with tears and sorrow. It was the day we watched our son's heartbeat stop on the ultrasound screen. God forgive me! I love him, please bring him home to you that I may see him another day.

CHAPTER 11

Christmas Present

My third pregnancy was not as I had anticipated after the reduction was completed. Soon after, I began to have regular frequent contractions that were placing me at high risk for preterm delivery. To prevent this from occurring I was instructed to remain on strict bed rest, given medications daily and strongly advised to avoid all sexual activity for the remainder of the pregnancy. This totaled about sixteen weeks.

These restrictions brought with them additional challenges that affected my entire family. I was still a midwifery student with only a few months till graduation and this setback was going to delay my completion of the program. Devin and Dax were still young enough that they needed their mom to be actively involved with them and not just a lump in a bed. Bedrest for me brought back flashbacks of my mother's marathon sleeping events during my early childhood. I didn't want my children to have these memories.

Larry was again burdened by increased family responsibilities that included being caregiver for me as well as the children. Overall, the pregnancy that in my mind offered promise of being "perfect" in comparison to my past pregnancies was not turning out the way I had planned. Each day, I feared that day might be the one that I lost our child. Each day I lay in bed feeling more depressed and inadequate as I failed my children by not being available for them and failed my husband by not being able to maintain an uncomplicated pregnancy.

As the Christmas season approached, I finally reached full-term status. I was due in the winter, however as with most women at the last stages of pregnancy, any day would do.

My obstetrician paroled me from bed rest Christmas Eve and I was able to celebrate the holidays with family, hugely pregnant and hugely uncomfortable. I was unquestionably very large since being restricted to bed, I had gained more than 70 pounds! Of course, this didn't stop me from celebrating Christmas Eve with extended family as I piled my dinner plate high with ham and mashed potatoes, the traditional Christmas Eve meal in our family.

Christmas Eve celebration was healing for me. I once again felt vital to my family and remained hopeful that our pregnancy was reaching a point where fear of loss was no longer consuming my consciousness.

Larry and I returned home with the children around 11 p.m. and hurried them off to bed as they awaited the arrival of Santa Claus the following morning. Within three hours of a sound sleep, I awoke to the sharpest most dreadful stomach pains I could recall.

"Oh shit!" I thought as I prepared myself for what was to come. Each cramp, each contraction came with a fury. Relentless, rhythmic waves accelerated from zero to sixty in less than two minutes.

All I could chant, all I could think was the mantra of women in labor the world over, "Why did I do this again?"

I hurriedly showered and blew my hair dry as the contractions intensified. The pressure in my vagina tripled and I could feel the baby dropping centimeter by centimeter in search of the exit. Still, I was determined to put on my make-up before heading to the hospital. Worst case scenario: I would deliver my child at home. I could do it. After all, I am a nurse.

After dressing and becoming more presentable, my next task was to wake the children and let them know the baby was going to arrive soon. This task brought much more challenge and frustration than I had anticipated. As the hour neared 3 a.m., my two young children awoke with the belief that Santa had just arrived and never expected to hear that Christmas needed to wait a while because mommy and daddy were going to the hospital to have a baby. The excitement that these two young children were soon going to have a new baby brother was strongly foreshadowed by the realization that Christmas was going to be postponed.

With that news, my two loveable children became instantly consumed with sadness, their eyes flooded with tears. In an attempt to diffuse this chaos, I began a mad frenzy of shaking wrapped Christmas gifts under the tree so that I could bring gifts to the hospital for them to open later in the day. I huffed and groaned and rocked through contractions in search of the treasures under the tree that might remedy the sadness of a Christmas tainted by the birth of a sibling. As soon as I bundled up a few gifts, we were off to the hospital.

Less than 90 minutes after our arrival at the hospital, Ian was born: seven pounds, 21 inches long. As I rested, recovered, and once again thanked God for this amazing blessing I couldn't help but wonder how could he weigh only seven pounds when I gained seventy? How was that possible?

Life was hectic after Ian's birth. I recovered from his delivery for a few weeks and then prepared to finish my master's studies. My professors and classmates were completely supportive during my pregnancy and recovery. I became a real-life case study that could be analyzed in the classroom. Time flew by and I graduated in the fall, just a few months behind my classmates.

I secured my dream job as a nurse midwife with an amazing obstetrician that helped pave the foundation of my clinical career. Like every other working Mom, I struggled to balance work and my personal life. Each morning I would wake up and transform via hairspray and make-up, putting on my mask. I went to work wearing "normal" on my face, but never feeling it in my soul. I was different. My childhood was different. My family life was different. But work was my escape. It was here that I exceled. I could pretend that I was normal and all the baggage of real life was left behind. Each woman who thanked me for my support as she struggled with her own birth empowered me and helped heal my ego. Work became my priority, to the detriment of my family.

Larry became the primary caregiver and housekeeper along with his own full-time job. I worked constantly. I would take holidays and overtime to supplement our household income not comprehending the considerable stress it was causing on my marriage. I didn't realize the burden I was placing on his shoulders at the time because I was so consumed with a job that was satisfying me on many levels. I enjoyed my work and looked forward every day to providing care for women with the added bonus of watching babies be born. I was blessed to wake up each day and be happy to go to work. I felt blessed, but unfortunately didn't recognize my selfishness at the same time.

I began to identify all the pain of my past as part of my strength toward healing others. Dysfunctional family life, emotional abuse, single motherhood… had purpose. My experiences provided me credibility when providing care to other women. Each of my pregnancies brought with it experience that would translate to another woman at some time during my career. Even the anguish of high-risk pregnancy, loss of a twin, and the sequelae of obstetric complications enhanced my ability to empathize with other woman in similar situations. It was during my early career that I began to embrace the pain I had endured and reframe it from a victim consciousness to one of power to heal others. I was increasingly able to view myself as a mentor to women in my community and an example of the ability to overcome profound challenges.

What I was unable to see during these years was that, as my business success grew, I was becoming more ego-driven and arrogant at home. Behavior which challenged my marriage and was causing what could be irreparable damage. Despite Larry trying to tell me what he was experiencing, I was too selfish to care.

I was successful and becoming more independent than I had ever been before. I was consumed with being and doing whatever I wanted to do regardless of how my spouse might feel about my choices. I came from poverty and abuse. After years of hard work, I had personal income, status, and I wasn't going to be denied what I wanted. Family vacations, nice clothes, and anything else that made me feel like I had finally arrived.

As my success grew, so did interest from male colleagues. It is a dangerous combination inflated ego and admiration from other suitors when you are married. A combination that often leads to a bad outcome. As my husband was falling on my priority list, our marriage was nearly lost.

CHAPTER 12

Blurred Lines
in the Workplace

As painful as it is to admit, there were a few tough marital years ahead despite my professional career doing well. Many days I didn't want to try anymore and to be honest Larry probably had many more days than me. During that time, I felt misunderstood and mistreated. I thought he did not want to appreciate my feelings or all the challenges I was going through. I did a lot of blaming toward a very good man that tried to make my dreams come true to the best of his ability. In hindsight, I know I was the primary problem, but during the madness I was far too angry and hostile to consider that possibility. Ego had replaced my childhood fear of abandonment and low self-esteem. Ego became the new Shadow which was driving me toward success but at what cost?

At work, my colleague and I had a close friendship that took a turn in the unhealthy direction. Criticism at home, unhappiness, petty disagreements, and my insatiable need to prove myself was too much for one husband. Roger was a safe substitute for me. He provided compliments and simple attention, plus he was married. I translated this attention into a fantasy man who would care about me without judgment. I was never physically

attracted to him and I think this was what made him appear
to be safe to me. I had no desire to begin a sexual relationship
with him, but I liked the flirtation.

My loneliness at home accelerated my enjoyment of Roger's
attention, even though I knew it was wrong. Roger became a
temporary substitute for emotional intimacy during the time
Larry and I were in disorder.

But like I previously stated, admiration from other suitors
during a troubled time in any marriage is a dangerous combination that almost always ends poorly. Another man found me
attractive, laughed at my jokes, and provided small spurts of
happy in an otherwise mundane existence.

This brief moment lasted only a few months and ended quite
abruptly when I had one of my many "Light-bulb" moments
during a conversation with Devin, an early teen, who was seeking
relationship advice from his mother, a person with whom he placed
trust. At that moment, I realized that I had no business offering
advice to my son if I was perpetuating lies in my own relationship.

I recognized that any form of attention from another man
really was infidelity. I knew I didn't want to be untrue to Larry.
I needed to decide if my marriage was salvageable or if it was
time for Larry and me to part ways. Regardless of my decision,
Roger was never a part of my plans for the future nor was I in his.
I shared these feelings with Roger the next time we spoke. He
seemed to accept my decision and I interpreted this as sincere.

My marriage was still unraveling at home, but I couldn't
avoid the inevitable conversation with Larry to determine where
our marriage was heading.

One evening when I returned home from work, I asked Larry
if we could speak. I dumped all of my unhappiness, frustration
and anger in an emotionally fueled monologue that lasted most

of the night. Larry did the same. We yelled, we cried and we almost threw in the towel more than once, but in the end we chose as a team to make the necessary changes to improve our marriage and to be better people.

Roger and I continued to work together without conflict for over a year before my relationship with him became bizarre. In that time, Larry and I had begun the welcome healing of our marriage and we devoted specific days each week to either private "date" nights or "family" nights as our way to balance both important components of our lives.

As my marriage improved, Roger's marriage deteriorated. In the beginning, I did not think too much about it, but in retrospect, by the end of our working relationship, I was able to see there was a line crossed at that time. My relationship with Roger transformed from a professional one to a pattern of sexual harassment.

The first sign that my working relationship with Roger was changing came when I returned from a long weekend away with Larry.

In the weeks before, Roger had begun to exhibit subtle signs suggesting he was jealous of my husband and the time I spent with him. Roger began discouraging me from going home after office hours, asking me to stay at hospital and spend time talking with him. Roger also began to make inappropriate comments about phone conversations he overheard me having with Larry, cementing my suspicion he was jealous.

I began to feel suffocated in a role that went far beyond that of a professional colleague. Initially, I brushed off Roger's criticisms, aware that he was unhappy in his personal life. He constantly complained about his wife and her ineptness. But, by the time Larry and I went on our get-away, I began to see more clearly the underlying issue that was bothering Roger.

When I shared stories with Roger about all the fun we had during that fantastic weekend, Roger's demeanor abruptly shifted. The best I can describe it is he suddenly transformed into a jealous boyfriend.

I pointed out to him that he was acting jealous. He paused for several seconds before admitting that he supposed he was jealous.

I was stunned by his comment. I thought, "Oh shit, this isn't good."

I replayed his recent change in behavior over and over again in my mind. What was I supposed to do? Roger and I worked together frequently and he had admitted being jealous of my relationship with my husband. In my mind, I again downplayed his feelings and chalked them off to his unhappiness with his wife. I convinced myself this event was really nothing serious and no further action was necessary.

Roger and I carried on with our work that day with nothing more said. I became careful to avoid sharing personal stories with Roger that might create further jealous feelings. I rationalized that even if Roger was jealous, those feelings would likely pass once he really began to see that being involved with me was no bargain.

In my mind, I was a screw up. I wasn't normal, therefore he would eventually see that his jealousy was misplaced. Let's face it, I have a more scandalous past than most women and so I rationalized that any infatuation he might feel was likely going to resolve itself.

Work continued and seasons passed, but Roger's infatuation was undiminished. I had learned early in this period that if I gave Roger the attention he wanted, it made a significant difference in good work days verses bad ones. Roger wanted attention from me that made him feel special. If I failed to give him the attention he expected, he would become irritable or pout, whining that I didn't like him anymore.

Greeting him with a daily hug and kiss when no other colleagues were nearby kept him content for a while. He never pressured me for more intimate sexual contact, but he had an expectation of frequent physical contact with me when we were alone. Occasionally, he would squeeze my bottom. The sexual comments were endless.

I felt trapped. I was working with a man who required me to fill a void in his personal life. I couldn't avoid him in the job I currently had. This was the job I worked so hard for, the job that made me so passionately happy. I saw no option but to endure.

Devin would soon be going to college and Larry and I were both working hard to prepare for retirement. So, I bargained with myself and rationalized that a few hugs and kisses were okay given the alternative of losing a job that I loved and an income my family depended on.

In addition to my stress at work, which I shared with no one, Larry and I were being challenged by some significant emotional and behavioral problems with Devin. I was being torn apart at home with a difficult child and reduced to being a nurse toy at work with a physician who couldn't shake his infatuation for me. Life really sucked, again.

It seemed the Shadow had returned and my hope for happily ever after was just a delusion. Life was becoming increasingly intolerable. I found the success I wanted. I achieved the goal, the job of my dreams but to what end? A marriage being stressed. Children struggling with developmental issues. And the only place where I felt good about myself, my workplace, was now my prison.

CHAPTER 13

The Shadow Returns

During the summer Devin graduated from high school and before his departure for college, I received a telephone call that changed our family dynamic in a profound way.

It was Mary, the mother of Devin's girlfriend, Anne. Anne had recently broken up with him. Mary said she had some serious concerns about Devin and needed to speak with me urgently.

I agreed and we met within a few hours. She said Devin was acting inappropriately and that she was very concerned about his safety. My heart sank. Adrenaline surged through my body and my chest began to ache, but I fought for composure, trying to control any expression of anxiety that might became apparent through my facial expression or outward physical tremors.

Mary said she had reason to believe that Devin was cutting himself and threatening to cause himself harm as a result of the break-up with Anne.

I sat paralyzed as I listened to the words, trying to process those actions in relationship to my child.

All I could utter was, "What?" and Mary repeated the story.

I had just spent the morning with Devin in a joint therapy session, sitting to his immediate right. There was no mention of him causing harm to himself, nor did I see any marks that appeared suspicious. The only logical explanation was that perhaps Devin was making up this story to make Anne feel guilty for their break-up and was trying to manipulate her emotions. I had no reason to believe he would actually harm himself, however I would consider he would try to create a drama for attention from Anne. We spoke a while longer and I expressed my thanks for her sincere concern, agreeing to let her know the outcome.

I returned home to find Devin watching television and appearing to be without any concern at the moment.

"Let me see your wrists," I demanded, interrupting his entertainment.

"What? Why?" he asked in a surprised voice, attempting to avoid my request.

"You heard me," I said firmly, my anxiety was quickly mixing with anger. I had just received information from a woman I barely knew that my son was harming himself.

Devin pulled up the long sleeves of his sweatshirt. There on each wrist were fresh wounds pink and raised, superficial but definitely self-inflicted. Residual blood remained on one wrist, probably from earlier that morning. The others appeared to be a week or so old.

"Dear God, IT IS TRUE!" I thought. "My son is cutting himself. What the hell is next?"

After I inspected his arms and the rest of his body, we had a long conversation about Devin's state of mind. I told him I was floored that I could sit next to my son in a therapist's office that he would pretend to be okay when actually he was harming himself without my knowledge. He was nearly 18 years old and, in my eyes, his future looked fabulous. So, why in the world would he be causing harm to himself? All the possibilities swirled through my mind, including the potential that he suffered from a mental illness like my mother.

My son was struggling, and my familiar pattern began to run in my mind again: It was because I was a failure as a mother.

Devin had always been my most challenging child. He was hyper-reactive as a toddler and never learned that "no" it means "no." He threw endless temper tantrums in his determination to get his own way. He was a head banger and in early childhood, he often had a large bruised knot on his forehead that was the symbol of demanding his own way. His siblings were more calm easygoing kids. Devin was the strong-willed stubborn one. With Devin, I always had to be alert for his sneakiness and deception. He gave Larry and me a challenge in his quest to always "get one over" on his parents.

Devin looked for loopholes when we gave him instructions that he didn't agree with. Here's a funny example that Larry and I frequently recall: One night we were heading out to dinner and the children were being cared for by my father, "Poppy" to his grandchildren. Each were given strict instructions that the kitchen was closed with the exception of fruit if they became hungry. They had finished dinner and if they wanted a snack we had grapes, bananas, and other fruit from which they could choose.

Dax was fine with this and Devin appeared fine, but no sooner did we leave, Devin made the executive decision that Skittles candy would be an acceptable fruit substitute. When Larry and I returned home to learn that Skittles were the snack Devin had chosen his rationale was, "Well I thought they would be okay because they are fruit flavored." Devin found his loophole and ran with it.

This is pretty much the story of his childhood. As he grew, the challenges for us as his parents grew as well. Of course, I loved him and I persevered, praying daily that he would grow

79

out of this behavior. Devin was evaluated by his pediatrician and never viewed as anything other than a hyper-reactive child.

No, he wasn't hyperactive. The diagnosis was hyper-reactive which is different. Devin was a great kid when all was going according to his plan, but when he had to shift gears and follow a path he didn't like, he would react in an inappropriate manner. I was encouraged to read books about the variety of personality types of children and to learn how to cope with his behavior. He never needed medications. As a matter of fact, he was a very good student and got along well in the classroom. This supported the diagnosis that I later learned was simple manipulative behavior, very much like my mother exhibited throughout most of my life.

By the time I learned about his self-destructive behavior, Devin had been accepted to four of the five colleges to which he had applied and would be leaving home in a few short months. I had little time to help a son who was obviously experiencing something seriously wrong. I had no experience with cutting and other self-destructive behavior; my best plan to cope was to begin intensive therapy right away as a family and individually. I needed to understand why he was behaving this way, so therapy seemed the best plan.

I tried my best to understand what was going through his mind and what our family could do to deal with this crisis. We spent several days a week in therapy either individually or as a family listening and speaking and crying, desperately trying to understand why and how to make Devin better. We might as well have moved into the therapist's office that summer, because it seemed that we spent more time there then at home. But Larry and I were committed to helping Devin overcome this destructive behavior as his departure for college quickly approached.

My gut told me that Devin was not ready to leave home and

be out of his family environment. I was worried that sending him off in that frame of mind could lead to disastrous consequences. Deep in my spirit, I was terrified he would try to kill himself. As mid-August approached, I told the therapist I thought Devin was not yet ready to leave home. The therapist disagreed.

"Devin needs to leave home and begin a fresh start away from his ex-girlfriend so he can heal," he said. "I understand your concerns, but they are unwarranted at this time. Devin needs to get away and see if he can shake off his behavior."

I debated this question for a few weeks. The pediatrician started him on a low dose anti-depressant just two weeks before transition to his college, a four-hour drive from home. I watched and waited, seeking signs of improvement, anything at all to suggest that Devin was in recovery phase. The best I could see he was not harming himself and it appeared he was looking forward to a new environment and all the change involved with college life. Maybe the therapist was right. Change could foster healing. So, September came and Devin was off to college. All we could do was hope for the best.

It was a nightmare for me with Devin being away from home. I don't think I slept two consecutive nights that fall, his freshman semester. He was a few hours from home and we spoke daily, but he was in a very bizarre emotional place and seemed to be unable to move out of his negative behavior.

Most of the time, he seemed detached and distant. I was very fearful that he was still harming himself and really had no way of assessing him when he was not living in our home. Devin claimed he was taking his anti-depressants as prescribed, but within a few weeks away, his behavior spiraled out of control.

I was at work one day when I called Devin to check on him. He started the conversation speaking very erratically about

Anne and her family and was even suggesting that he was going to cause them harm. I frantically tried to process his words and determine if this was detached anger or a seemingly sincere statement and a legitimate warning of his intent to harm them.

As Devin continued to speak rapidly, barely taking a breath he sounded more and more erratic and unstable. All I could think was, "Oh dear God, what do I do? What do I do?"

I scrambled in my mind to develop a plan to manage this child and figure out why he was falling apart. When he finally completed his monologue filled with rage toward Anne's family, I begged him to stay put in his room and told him I was coming to visit him just as soon as I finished seeing patients. My job was actually an hour closer to him than my home, so it wouldn't take as long.

He agreed he wouldn't go anywhere, so I rushed to finish my work day and get to my son, who was obviously falling apart. I also called Larry and asked him to speak with Devin and do his own assessment of Devin's state of mind, hoping that perhaps I was just over-exaggerating and my son wasn't so bad after all. I tried to hold on to a glimmer of hope that maybe I was just overreacting and Larry would reassure me that Devin was just fine.

No such luck this time. Larry agreed that Devin appeared to be seriously irrational and that he needed immediate help. We decided to phone the college's emergency hotline that was intended to address issues such as this and advise them of the situation and that I was en route.

The people working with the hotline were very patient and reassuring. By the time I had reached Devin's dorm room they were already there, speaking with him along with the local police who were called for assistance.

I could see at the first glance that Devin was in a seriously bad frame of mind and we all agreed he needed a prompt psychiatric evaluation. Devin's eyes were dark and hollow. His expression was empty, detached and devoid of emotion. I could see my son losing touch with reality right before my eyes while I stood helpless and fearful.

Eight hours later, an evaluation by a team of mental health experts provided some answer to Devin's behavior. The most encouraging of the news was that Devin was extremely unlikely to harm anyone. The experts decided that Devin's rant about harming Anne or her family was nothing more than a young man with an attitude problem who wasn't able to manipulate people and get his own way.

We knew from the summer's counseling sessions that Devin was hurting because of the breakup and, because he felt pain, he was in turn trying to cause Anne and her family pain by making false threats.

In a nutshell, he wasn't getting his own way, so he was escalating his manipulation to a level that he thought would bring Anne back to him. Unfortunately, he was unable to recognize the consequences were going to be much more harmful to him and he didn't recognize that manipulation rarely gets the results he was seeking. This was pretty much Devin's theme during his childhood. He was a great kid when things went his way and impossible to deal with when they didn't.

I was completely exhausted, physically and mentally. As dawn neared after a night of sitting in the waiting room of a psychiatric facility waiting for what I feared was a diagnosis of doom, I could not accept that my son was manipulating and that this behavior was calculated.

"Are you sure he is not bipolar or schizophrenic?" I asked.

There had to be a more organic cause of why someone would behave so erratically and detached manner.

"No, Ms. Lamar, your son is a troubled young man who needs to accept that life isn't always going to go the direction he expects it should," the doctors told me.

At dawn, Devin was released to my care, still taking the same anti-depressant and under the advice that he needed to begin weekly therapy to learn better coping skills. Certainly, this was a much better diagnosis than a mental illness, but I was still questioning how my child could behave in such an extreme manner simply because he wasn't getting what he wanted.

I drove Devin home and we all spent the weekend recovering from fatigue. I just wanted to decompress, understand why this was happening, and most importantly make it stop.

I was very fortunate to reach out to Dr. Z, a local psychiatrist, who was willing to meet with Devin on a weekly basis and provide guidance to all of us. Devin began weekly visits with Dr. Z as he resumed college the following Monday. He took a three hour-long bus ride each way to his weekly appointment with the doctor. Larry and I struggled throughout the semester allowing Devin to remain at school, but the professionals believed that was the best plan for the moment.

My new "normal" became weekly long-distance visits to my son, picking him up at the bus station to bring to and from his psychiatrist appointments and trying to appear pleasant at work each day as well as being wife and mother at home to the other two children who didn't understand this madness.

Unfortunately, my other children suffered the most. Although I was able to muddle through work, I really had no energetic reserves by the time I got home. By the early winter, I was juggling the family challenge of a very troubled son with trying to balance my family life and be a wife and mother to my other children who were experiencing the consequences of their brother's instability.

In addition, I was being more and more challenged by Roger and trying to find ways out of working directly with him by asking other nurse colleagues to exchange patient assignments with me without drawing attention to my situation. On the labor floor with so many curious people, I had no doubt it would not take long for that attention to come.

Roger appeared pleasant in front of others; however he would seek out private time with me where he would behave more flirtatiously as he continued his ridiculous and unwanted pursuit. His relentless behavior was making it impossible for me to function professionally. Almost like a jealous suitor, he demanded my personal attention, including hugs and flirtatious behavior whenever he could get me alone.

I was trapped. My obligation to my children required all I could give as a mother to help Devin through his crisis and provide stability to the best of my ability for Dax and Ian.

At the same time, I was under enormous pressure to be a play toy for a physician who was very well respected in our community. Roger tried to fill the void of an unhappy home life with this workplace flirtation to be that had become an obsession.

I had no refuge. I had no space and no opportunity to escape from the daily pressure of my life to take care of myself and my own needs. Quite frankly during that time, I did not even have the time to recognize that I had needs. I was consumed by stress, fear, guilt and several other unnamed emotions that affect a mother challenged by an emotionally unhealthy child. I was entirely consumed with my efforts to help him heal and protect my other children. Somehow, unbelievably, it never occurred to me to turn to Larry for solace.

Something had to give, so at work it was just easiest to give Roger what he wanted. I once again became an actress. I put on a mask and I pretended by giving the empty hugs and empty flirtation that he expected while at work. I had no energy left to try to resolve that issue. In fact, I knew in my inner being, in my core, I couldn't resolve this issue. He was a physician. I was just a nurse. His job was more valuable than mine and given a choice, I was the expendable one. Roger wanted my attention and I needed my job, even more so in a time of family crisis.

During that time, I was very much like the actress I had become the afternoon so many years ago when I engaged in that humiliating sexual act as a means to win the return of my absconded child, my baby Devin.

There I was, nearly twenty years later, pretending to be something I wasn't in order to secure my position within a workplace that held me at its mercy. I needed my income and was in no position to give it up. A nurse reporting inappropriate behavior by a physician was the kiss of death. I would most definitely lose my job one way or another and would very likely not find another one in my small community.

So, in my mind, I justified my behavior and told myself it was okay. I hugged Roger every time he wanted it, in a desperate effort to make my work life more tolerable. That attention seemed to keep him satisfied for a while, so I played the role. During my drive from home to work every day, I'd have to psyche myself up to assume my role as the "other me," the "nurse toy." Larry and the rest of my family had no idea of my dual life.

I tried to detach from my home stress and prepare for my day at the hospital where, if Roger was not working, it would be a good day. If he was working I would do what it took to keep him happy just for a little peace. At the time, it seemed a small price to pay for the salary that my family needed as we became more and more challenged by medical bills. I was wife, mother, nurse and actress. Perhaps actress was my first role.

Looking back, the Shadow that was my world was in complete control. Everything I thought I had overcome had never really left. I was drowning in Darkness. I was going to be better than my mother. I was going to be the best wife I could be and I was going to be the best midwife. I needed to be everything I thought I was supposed to be. Yet, everything I was supposed to be, everything I was striving to become, was being challenged by obstacles that I could not overcome. I was failing as a mother, as a wife, and as a nurse, therefore I was failing myself. I couldn't understand what the purpose of being was and even came to a point of questioning God's existence.

I felt empty. I was devoid of faith and desperately hanging on through the only survival skill that worked for me, manipulation. Funny, that is what Devin did, too. I wonder where he learned that....

It was through my inherent survival skill of manipulation that I was trying to make the best of my work situation. I was once again the "actress" playing the role of making a man in my life happy by giving him the attention he demanded. I was leaving work only to return home and be the "actress" to my husband and children pretending that work went well and life was good as I desperately strove to create a family life that portrayed some sense of normalcy. I was actress to the patients, giving truly sound advice to each woman encouraging, empowering and lifting them up to be strong, healthy, happy individuals. I was supporting them in labor as they worked hard to become mothers while I questioned my own maternal abilities so deeply.

It was all a lie. I was living a lie. Clinging to my fantasy of normalcy that I wanted so desperately to come to fruition. In the end though, the act became so confusing, convoluted that even I couldn't discern what truth was. I was the lie.

CHAPTER 14

The Shadow Defined

A life in persistent chaos does not necessarily define chaos as bad. A busy family that juggles children, work, sports, music, and pets is chaotic, but when the energy of the family is mutually supportive and aligned to meet the daily goals then chaos is controlled, even accepted. My world was no longer being fueled by controlled chaos of a busy family, it had transmuted to dense Shadow which consisted of energies of manipulation, emotional and physical abuse, and sexual mistreatment. An uncontrolled dense Shadow has the ability to become its own entity, a Poltergeist which drains all the happy out of the environment and people around it.

This is what happened in my home. A Poltergeist had formed. The consequence of adults who proved incapable of coping with stressors in a healthy manner. I had painfully demonstrated that my coping skills were negligible, but my husbands were challenged as well. His mid-western upbringing makes him a gentleman to a fault, but nobody is prepared to manage the multitude of trials our family experienced that seemingly poured down upon us in a steady storm for more than three years.

A frail marriage, an eldest child trying to cope with feelings of inadequacy due to parental abandonment, all compounded by my unacknowledged workplace incivility proved unbearable. The Poltergeist rooted in my home and sucked the energy of love and happy out. It drained the joy from my family as it drained my Light and mocked me in the process. Each day reminding me that I was a failure, undeserving of anything but pain. In my home no Light shined and drama ruled, the Poltergeist was taking charge.

I just existed each day, a prisoner at home and a prisoner at work. My sanctuary, sacred space, felt oppressive and I had no faith within me that the Light would return. I had no hope. My days of faith and feeling the presence of God in my world were gone.

The miracle of birth had sadly become a job. Climbing into bed with the man I adored was just another night of escape into my dream state where I could run from all Darkness and hope I didn't wake up.

That is a difficult truth for any Starseed to admit. In my discussions with others, they recall similar breaking points where the Darkness seemed to be winning and human life felt too hard to continue with. Hope was reduced to hoping not to wake up because being alive hurt too much. My family had been enduring pain for several years and I didn't know the worst was still before us. I had no faith to sustain.

I had yet to sort out that I was experiencing workplace harassment. I couldn't diagnose it for myself. I could have for any patient or friend, but for me I couldn't name the behavior of my colleague as harassing. That lightbulb moment was still in the distance and would be the metaphoric breaking point of my life that forever transformed me. Providing the tools necessary to heal myself and the relationships around me.

Many critics ask why I didn't promptly report sexually

inappropriate behavior and hostility immediately to my superiors. This is certainly a fair and reasonable question. The best answer I can offer is that he was a physician and I am not.

In healthcare, there is a Shadow that has for decades turned a blind eye to physician indiscretions including inappropriate physical touch and sexually inappropriate or even demeaning comments. It is such a norm that it took me more than a year to finally identify that what I was experiencing was mistreatment.

However, once I acknowledged it to myself, I was certain that any form of reporting would only be to my detriment. I would never be believed. He would be protected and I would be unemployed. I needed my job. My income was vital to my family lifestyle and I had to learn how to cope. I knew what he was doing was wrong, but I needed my job. I loved my job, at least up that point. Oh yes, there were those cold winter days where climbing out of warm blankets was the absolute last thing I wanted to do. Nevertheless, I always loved my job.

I am a nurse midwife. All I ever wanted to do was empower women on their life's journey. I was born into powerless circumstances, yet it seemed natural my desire to join in a healing profession. I am a proud nurse. Overcoming childhood adversity and obstacles in my personal life left me with a feeling that I was well suited to counsel other women on their paths. Armed with this philosophy, I carried on and tried to endure. No conscious thought yet to be considered about one's mission and purpose in life or Light vs Dark. I was faithless and navigating Darkness seemingly on my own.

My workplace was increasingly becoming a prison for me rather than a medical healing environment. The more Roger reported being unhappy at home, the more he expected me to fill that void. Secret hugs and kisses shared during work hours.

He seemed to love the forbidden thrill that came with almost being caught by others. I just wanted to die.

I was trapped.

Every time I tried to avoid his leer or his touch, he became offended and gave me not-so-subtle signals of his disapproval. My one-time dream job had turned into a prison. I watched the clock as each patient came in and came out. By the end of my work day, I would grab my car keys and plan my hasty exit. Years passed as I tried to make the best of a bad situation. I never realized how much I was enduring until the nightmare finally reached its climax. My failure to recognize the seriousness of my situation distresses me almost as much as the horror story that was unfolding day by day.

I knew that I was struggling. I knew things weren't right, but I kept convincing myself that I could work it out. I believed that Roger's attraction was destined to fizzle out and that he would eventually leave me alone. I believed that if I ignored him long enough, he would finally get the message. I continued justifying the bad situation in so many ways.

Throughout the interminable legal process that was to follow, I was often asked, "Why?" Why didn't I quit my job? Why didn't I report Roger? Why didn't I do a thousand things to stop the pain?

There was only one answer: I needed my job. I was earning good money and I had a family to support. I was paying a mortgage. I was paying for three growing children. I needed my job. Reporting a physician would be a permanent red flag on my resume. I was never going to find a job like that again in my community. I had a responsibility to my family. So I endured.

I think on another level I somehow believe that I deserved this kind of living hell. I was not worthy of healthy relationships.

Shadow had convinced me I had no worth. So I would put on my daily mask of normal and pretend.

Days droned on and work life was becoming increasingly unbearable. Work works reached a climax within days of returning from a few days off with Larry. I was rested and in good spirits, ready to get back to business. Roger was not so happy. Within hours of my return to the labor floor, he bombarded me with insults about taking time off to be with my husband.

Initially, I ignored his comment, trying to process why he was in such a foul mood. I never did figure out why he was so upset, but his knowledge that I was away with my husband was very upsetting to him and he wanted me to know it.

Roger started a new tactic: insulting my husband. His new approach was what he thought was flattery: that I had married beneath me and that I deserved better. My head began to spin as I tried to defend myself and my marriage, to no avail. I was furious. He had crossed a line. I knew for certain he was wrong, but I also knew that proving Roger wrong wasn't going to end this fight. He was absolute in his conviction, but I knew better that he was really upset because I had been away with Larry again.

OH DEAR GOD! HOW DID I GET MYSELF INTO THIS POSITION?

The tone of the conversation with Roger escalated as I stood firm, defending myself, fully understanding it was likely making the situation worse. I was so angry that I just didn't care. He wanted my attention. He wanted my time. He wanted me to replace all the unhappiness in his life.

I was sick of it. I wanted my boundaries back. I wanted to stop having to satisfy his need for relationship. Somehow the boundaries were all blurred. It was time for me to regain control of my body and my role in my workplace. I knew that once I made this decision, in the end it would cost me my job. I didn't care anymore. I had enough. He had crossed the line that forced my hand.

"F him!" I thought, outraged by his gall in passing judgment on my marriage, my family, or my choices. How dare he continue to violate my body and my personal space making it impossible for me to function in a healthy and safe work environment. I was furious.

How did I let this happen? I just did.

Our argument continued for what seemed like hours when suddenly Roger's demeanor changed from hostile and overbearing to one of a pouting small boy. I guess he realized that this argument was pushing me very far away from him. Maybe it was embarrassment or concern that I would report him. Maybe it was because I finally stood up to him, but his personality shifted and he began to back pedal from the confrontation.

My mind raced at supersonic speed. I was in a tailspin. I immediately realized, "OH, MY GOD! I am right. Think, Stacey. Now what?"

I settled my tone and my posture down to a calm that I didn't feel. I looked at him as if the fight had never happened.

I shrugged my shoulders and left the room.

I returned to the nurse's locker room and closed the bathroom door. My heart was racing, my body shaking as I replayed the events that I had just endured. I looked up to heaven and thought, "This just can't be happening."

But it was.

During that period, it seemed I needed to prove to myself that my theory was correct. Roger liked me too much and I needed to get help with this problem. But how?

I was painfully cautious not to draw my coworkers' attention to myself and Roger. In their eyes, all was status quo and Roger and I were simply friends. I wear a good mask of normal since I have a lifetime of practice. No one would believe that anything unscrupulous was happening behind the scenes.

If I heard this same story from a friend, I could have easily analyzed the situation and advised her that she was being mistreated, even sexually harassed. But I couldn't see it in my own situation. In hindsight, I can now see that I didn't have enough self-worth to recognize the extent of Roger's abuse. I had been emotionally and physically abused all throughout my childhood. I had learned to behave according to the standard of the environment I was in, just to "fit in." Roger wanted me to behave a certain way, so I did. If I made him happy then work went well. So, I just did.

CHAPTER 15

The Ugly Truth about Workplace Harassment

Sexual harassment at work is a debilitating problem that for the victim often leads to a no-win situation. In my case, I didn't even identify Roger's inappropriate behavior as sexually harassing for more than a year. I knew I was being bullied and I knew that he was becoming more and more out of control, but I kept believing that if I persevered I could get control of this situation and make it better. The social norm of sexual banter and rude or inappropriate comments has been part of the healthcare setting for decades. I began in that environment in the 80s and never witnessed disciplinary action despite being observer to some pretty vulgar exchanges.

Being sexually harassed by a person with higher authority is even more problematic because the victim is being mistreated by the very person who is has direct power over them. Persistent mistreatment left unresolved will eventually result in the victim becoming worn down physically, emotionally and spiritually.

The stress I was experiencing at work led to physical symptoms such as insomnia and stomach aches from anxiety and anticipation of what the day would bring. I drove to work in a perpetual state of doom plotting my course to keep out of Roger's sight as much as possible.

He had grown accustomed to hugs and flirtation and it was becoming more and more difficult to dodge his advances. No matter what I did, it was becoming more apparent that my efforts to diffuse Roger's inappropriate behavior were futile.

I changed my routine, switched days off with coworkers, anything I could think of to avoid contact with Roger. I thought this would discourage his advances. However, the more I avoided him, the angrier and more belligerent he became. It became impossible to focus on my work responsibilities and patients who depended upon me for their lives and those of their babies.

Patient care suffered as I became more and more distracted attempting to avoid conflict. I felt stalked every time I was on the labor floor and he was there with one of his office patients. I was constantly "on guard." He enjoyed the thrill of the pursuit, the secrecy and I was the target. I was the nurse toy and as such I was expected to put him first on my priority list and to behave in ways that satisfied him. This included sharing meals, hugs, kisses and other secret flirtatious behavior.

Each day that I tried to avoid this contact and reclaim my personal space was a day that I would face private retribution for not complying with his wishes. It was as if I had been unknowingly groomed to meet his needs and when I finally realized this was happening, it was too late to escape. I was trapped.

Each time I avoided physical or emotional contact with him, Roger would behave like a wounded adolescent boy who couldn't get over his crush. I was in a hopeless situation. No matter how I tried to overcome it, I was drowning. As busy as we were with patient care, Roger was still able to remain distracted with me as he maintained this unhealthy need to know my personal business. He was consumed with me in our workplace.

The workplace Shadow grew along with my sense of doom as I continued to get through patient hours and hustle home to my house of horrors. To add to my profound isolation, I had never once shared with Larry what I was experiencing at work. I had no idea how to explain it or where to begin trying to share what I was enduring at work. I didn't understand it myself.

I was afraid. Roger was becoming increasingly irrational in his behavior toward me. He was saying very inappropriate things about his wife that included violence and I was very much in fear for my personal safety. I didn't feel strong enough to share any of this experience with my husband. So, as always, I endured.

By the end of one particular day filled with adolescent jealousy toward my personal time with Larry, I had reached my limit. The harassment had to end. It was apparent to me in the way he switched off his anger that I was being manipulated very much like the behavior of Devin.

This was it. By the afternoon, I summoned the courage to place the call that I knew would likely end my career. I phoned the hospital director and prayed for help as the call connected. I was hoping that this conversation might have a better outcome than I had anticipated. I feared retaliation. Yet I prayed I was wrong.

The conversation was brief, but emotionally charged. I was uncontrollably crying and quite desperate as I requested a meeting as soon as possible to discuss a problem I was having. I was very clear this was not appropriate to speak about over the phone and that I would like to schedule a personal meeting. The secretary assured me she would relay the message to the director and he would be in contact with me. He never called.

Two weeks passed with no return phone call. I knew I was doomed. I continued to endure.

During this time, I learned that I was not the first nurse to complain about Roger. As a matter of fact, as the legal process unfolded years later, I learned the list was longer than I could have imagined. In previous hospitals he had worked at similar complaints were lodged and none of the women who accused Roger of inappropriate behavior had remained in their jobs.

Yet Roger remained employed. He was a very good physician and was vital to business operations and revenue. There is no doubt in my mind that the Director learned of the anxiety in my voice in that very brief phone conversation. He had no idea the depth of the complaints I planned to share with him. It was this calculated disinterest that assured me that I was doomed. Roger was going to be protected. I was expendable.

I reached deep into my soul to find the resolve to carry on and make the best of a bad situation. The bottom line was unchanged; I needed my income, so I had no choice but to persevere.

In just a few short weeks, it seemed that the Universe was going to take charge and remove me from this unhealthy environment. I didn't have the emotional strength or fortitude to protect myself. Just when it seemed that I would "emotionally break" one day from the incredible stress at work, I sustained the unforeseen injury that immediately changed the path of career and my future. I was at the end of my rope, wrought with fear and stress from boss and during a routine vaginal birth my body "physically snapped". The popping sound was audible to everyone in the room. For a brief moment, I believed the infant's clavicle must have fractured during the birth process, but almost instantly my left hand was on fire with a burning pain. I could barely rotate appropriately to do the required maneuvers to safely deliver this newborn that was racing to his finish line. I fought through the extreme pain, safely delivered an amazing new life to a wonderful family and proceeded to the emergency room to assess what type of injury I sustained.

It was in that moment that my injury forcibly removed me from a hostile and abusive work environment. In hindsight, my physical self protected me from the greater issues by forcing my life into a pause. As strange as it may seem to some, I truly believe that if my body didn't literally break that very day something much worse could have happened to me in the near future. I was being rescued from a situation that I couldn't rescue myself from.

With a broken hand, I was forced to remove myself from this secretly unhealthy environment and face my circumstances. The overpowering fear I had of Roger was becoming suffocating. The was still no communication from the superior I reached out to for a conversation and guidance. I was being ignored for concerns about what I had to say. But now, I was injured and I required surgery which proved to be more complex than anticipated and my recovery turned out to be much longer than expected.

This situation was becoming larger than I could process and I was becoming increasingly despondent. I sought counsel from an outside source. After a few weeks, I drew the courage to contact an attorney and share my story.

Initially, I spoke to an attorney about my injury and my rights under worker's compensation law. I knew in the back of my mind I wanted to share the darker issue I was experiencing, but I was afraid to speak. Feeling confused and truly helpless, I was terrified to tell somebody my story even though I finally had an opportunity to be heard. Before our meeting ended, I very cautiously mentioned that I had something else I would like to discuss and asked her if she had the time.

I slowly and in great detail shared with him the events of the past few years at work. He listened carefully, interrupting my story once in a while to gain clarity where he felt it was necessary. At the end of my narrative, he diagnosed my case: "Stacey, you are being sexually harassed."

It still amazes me; I live and relive painful and humiliating events, that until that lawyer's pronouncement I never placed a name on my hell in the workplace. I knew Roger's behavior was wrong; I knew it was unacceptable; I knew it was inappropriate, but I had not been able to see it for what it truly was: sexual harassment and intimidation.

A multitude of emotions swept over me as I pondered my lawyer's words. I knew that I was at the end of my rope, that I could no longer be subjected to Roger's increasingly irrational behavior. I had tried to communicate with my hospital's executives about what I was experiencing, but I got a very clear message when they failed to return my calls or to schedule promised meetings. I was desperate for someone to hear me, but no one would listen.

My attorney remained empathetic about my plight, but he clearly spoke of sexual harassment through the lens of the legal system. He warned me that this would not be an easy journey. Sexual harassment victims are often treated like rape victims. I could expect to be accused of "asking for it." I wasn't sure if I had the emotional stamina to proceed.

But before I could consider going any further legally, I needed to share with Larry what I had been experiencing for the past few years. I had to share the current story and I had to share the past. Larry had absolutely no idea what I was experiencing at work.

He and the children would complain that I was coming home irritable and completely unapproachable. Yet, they had no idea the challenges I was experiencing. I blamed myself for this chaos and the fact that the brief emotional relationship from years earlier somehow contributed to my present troubles. I had to share everything with Larry and release it from my soul. I was holding on to this dark, dirty secret that seemed to be rotting a part of me and contributing to our marital discord.

I prayed for courage to a God I was uncertain cared as I prepared to share this hidden story with the man I truly loved. I knew I had made a profound mistake. I had created a mountainous lie.

Larry listened. He was angry and I am certain he felt betrayed, although he never specifically told me so. He asked many questions and formulated his own theory. I answered everything with honestly and with deep sorrow for the hurt I had caused him and our family. In the end, he forgave me.

I returned to work several weeks later on limited duty as I continued to heal, but I was needed at work to assist my coworkers in an administrative capacity. It took only a week for Roger's sexual flirtation to resume. My anxiety once more became more than I could handle. Work became so unbearable that I was forced to make a decision to either stay and potentially lose my mind or to leave and bring the issue to the court.

I chose the latter.

I sought personal counsel from Dr. Z and he advised me to leave work and documented "hostile work environment." With that note, the train of the legal process left the proverbial station. I was setting out for the ride of my life.

The lawsuit began the following winter with the support of my husband and with the instruction of speaking to no one about the ongoing litigation. My employer assumed no responsibility and ultimately defended the honor of their physician. The wheels of justice move slowly and it took nearly two years for depositions to be completed. The legal process began somewhere in 2009-10 and I attended each deposition as a testament to my truth and my need to be present against those that sought to destroy my reputation. Not one executive would even make eye contact me. I was a colleague. A reputable employee. A loyal provider of safe community care and I was punished for calling out bad behavior and not accepting an inside deal. I was the enemy. I believe that, despite their culpability they hoped I would just go away. It would unquestionably have been easier for me to drop it. But, that would make me a quitter and would bring victory to perpetrator. I wanted accountability for failing to protect me and for ignoring me when I was desperately seeking help. But, I also wanted my truth to be heard with the goal of preventing another victim down the road. A financial payoff would be perceived as showing my interest only in the money. This never aligned with my soul's truth. I needed to stand firm and face the people who took away my joy and my happiness. I couldn't give up. I had to accept the deafening silence of the legal process, forbidden to speak with others less my husband and legal or medical professionals.

With the start of the legal process came deep and profound isolation that I would endure for the next few years. Coworkers quickly learned that Roger and I were not getting along. I had suddenly stopped working because I was being treated for my broken hand. In my absence the gossip began. Some colleagues had theories and personal opinions that they shared with me, but I never spoke about the depth of my personal experience.

Rumors began to fly. A few confided in me that they believed Roger treated me like a wife. They further posited that he was "in love with me and upset because he couldn't have me." I was even told there was an ongoing office wager about who would win the lawsuit. My pain became workplace fodder during the years that pre-date the social movement #metoo and the public rebuke of inappropriate behaviors of prominent figures that began to shine Light on this Shadow of social oppression that had been normalized. Sadly, the Shadow lives in healthcare too and the legal judgments of my journey define the inequalities that live on.

As my legal process continued, the incredible naivete of mine was revealed which began my awakening of consciousness that I am Light. I was disillusioned with the power of deposition under oath and the obligation to tell the truth. I had a natural assumption that no one would put their hand on the Bible and be dishonest. It seems fantastic that I was this gullible given my childhood and history. But, I was and I learned quickly that the legal oath was not a guarantee of truthfulness. I also learned quickly that others being questioned, despite their knowledge, needed their jobs and were also in fear, therefore truth was not absolute.

I was left on my own to defend myself without anyone else stepping up to speak on my behalf. As the legal process unfolded, hospital staff and executives all seemed to develop amnesia. As depositions continued, I wish I had a dollar for the hundreds, if not thousands, of times I heard very bright, educated people respond to simple questions with, "I don't recall."

Time and time again, any question that offered even the simplest vindication on my behalf was answered by, "I don't recall."

I was defeated. Emotionally, physically, and spiritually drained. Fear of retaliation was fueled by repetitive denial and implicit dishonesty further Darkening each day, making it more and more challenging to just breathe.

My attorney told me frankly that I was going to be treated like the "rape victim who deserved it." I kept trying to hold onto the belief that, in the end, people would know that I was telling the truth. I was foolish enough to believe that the truth always prevails.

I got an occasional phone call from former co-workers who would share work news with me and update me on other hospital gossip. Eventually the calls stopped coming and the hospital family with which I spent five years bonding was fading to a memory. I was disposable. Colleagues needed to move on and protect themselves, yet I believed one day my truth would be revealed and friendships restored. In the meantime, the Shadow of isolation continued.

The result was traumatic. I am a wife, a mother and a nurse. Yet, because I was broken, physically, emotionally and spiritually, I had lost a large part of my identity. A large part of me, my ego, was the fact that I was a nurse. Much of what enriched my life was my being with and caring for women in my community. I thrived and healed myself as I healed others in this role.

I had left work each night feeling satisfied because I had been able to spend that day helping other women. Whether it was a simple labor check or an absolutely back-breaking labor, I mattered because I was able to support others.

Suddenly it was all gone. Once again, I had allowed a man to control me and weaken me and take from me what I held so dear. He took part of my ego and part of my soul. I didn't have the life skills to recognize it as it was taking place and I didn't have the life skills to stop him. I could counsel patients to make sound choices, but I couldn't make sound choices for myself.

My life as I knew it crumbled as I fell into Darkness. Rumors and gossip spread through the community and I was forced to remain silent, indefensible. If for nothing else then to preserve the integrity of my legal case. I wasn't going to hit low. The legal system would prevail. Light will prevail. That was my truth and it had to sustain me.

But in truth, I was heartbroken, ashamed and humiliated. I was unable to protect myself because I didn't have sound judgment in my arsenal. Continuing complications from my broken hand prevented me from working. I was emotionally distraught and spent most days crying. I tried really hard remain strong in front of my children, but I couldn't always stop myself. I went to the psychiatrist every couple of weeks and would call in between scheduled appointments if I couldn't make it through. My psychiatrist, my husband and my attorney were the only people I could speak with. So, I sat at home and cried on the in between days waiting for my next appointment.

CHAPTER 16

The Shadow
of Isolation

In our sessions, Dr. Z sometimes referred to himself as the "the country shrink." I think this was his way of injecting some humor into an hour-long visit filled with some pretty painful emotions.

I began seeing Dr. Z when Devin was in his teenage meltdown in 2007. He was a community physician with a very good reputation. I knew him through hospital events, but was hesitant to share the level of dysfunction in my family. But, I needed help so I took the chance.

Given his reputation, I felt he was the best person I could find to help with my family problems. I shared our drama with him and he agreed to start evaluating and treating my family. As with the treatment of any minor child, the parents will eventually become involved in the evaluative process and that was fine. Dr. Z helped all of us to overcome Devin's tribulations most importantly, Devin overcame is shadow and works with others to empower them.

When I couldn't take any more abuse at work, I turned to him again.

It seemed more than fate the day I ran into Dr. Z in the

hospital hallway while I was still working at the hospital. I had been contemplating phoning him and trying think of how to broach the subject when one morning, there he was approaching me in a quiet hallway. As discreetly as possible, I tried to explain to him that I was in a very bad situation at work that involved Roger and I was feeling desperate. I recall asking him specifically if discussing this type of issue would be a problem for him because Roger was his colleague, too. I feared that perhaps Dr. Z might not want to accept me as a patient because of the professional relationship he had with Roger. He understood my concern and stated that because he had treated me before he had no issue that would prevent him from treating me with my current dilemma.

I also remember telling Dr. Z that if he would not treat me, I probably would not seek care elsewhere. The thought of starting treatment with a new therapist to me was more than I could handle during that trying time. Dr. Z knew my family dynamics; he knew my personal dynamics and he knew the infrastructure of the hospital I worked for and he knew Roger. I believed he was the best qualified to help me. Thankfully, he agreed. That chance meeting occurred only weeks before I left my job under the escalating hostility in my work environment.

I started treatment promptly and struggled to make it through each week until the next scheduled session. Every two weeks, Dr. Z listened intently to my story. I felt validated. He gave me sound words of advice and allowed me to challenge his thinking when I didn't quite agree. Most importantly, he began to show me the interconnectedness between my childhood and the harassment I had endured from Roger in a way that made sense to me.

In a nutshell, I began to understand that we are not born with the skills to protect ourselves from predators. Our family members and significant role models mentor us and teach us how to recognize unhealthy situations. In my case, I was not mentored during my childhood or anytime. I had no one to teach me how to protect myself from people who mistreated me.

Quite the contrary, Dr. Z showed me that I was not only a victim of emotional and physical abuse as an adult, but that my entire childhood was one of persistent child abuse. I didn't have the occasional bad day growing up. I had the occasional good one.

Everyone from my mother to relatives to teachers had failed to protect me. They knocked me down every step of the way. The only person I could lean on was my father. However, my father enabled my abusers by failing to see just how bad it was for me.

By the time I reached young adulthood, I had developed no internal skills to protect me from people who meant me harm. Furthermore, as my part of the coping skills I developed, I would often "dumb down" or not be myself in order to fit in with the crowd. I so desperately wanted to fit in that I would become a chameleon just so I would be liked.

This was the norm in my work environment by the time the abuse had reached its crescendo. I was perpetually trying to "fit in" with Roger, to please him by being what he expected me to be rather than being what I truly was and who I wanted to be. Religion had been an early component of my development and religion was a factor in my abuse as well. During the course of my therapy, I developed some clarity about the negative impact religion had on me during my formative years and during my Dark journey.

Therapy continued as I struggled with loneliness, depression and anxiety. I was overcome with shame and the belief that I was a profound failure as a wife and mother.

Dr. Z counseled me and helped me to put my emotions into perspective, but those hour-long sessions passed quickly and it was in the many other hours of isolation and despair that I reflected alone.

I would go deep into my childhood and try to piece the jigsaw puzzle of my life together just like Dr. Z would do. I would try to connect events and process patterns and then bring these patterns to Dr. Z at my next session where he would either confirm them or dismiss them with a different and frequently more accurate explanation.

In the Darkness was my silence and in the silence was my healing. I didn't know what the healing was yet, but I knew that there were lessons on my horizon that I must learn to heal. I could feel that there were messages unique to me designed to feed my Higher Self. Divine knowing that would guide me through the Darkness so that I would someday feel my Light again.

My faithful dog, Simon endured with me during the first year of my legal isolation. Our family dog, the seven-year old Bichon had been my Valentine's Day gift when he was just a puppy. He was a great family dog and my loyal friend. In between therapy visits Simon was on deck listening to me every day as I spoke out loud to him about all my troubles. He laid by me when I cried and never passed judgment on me when I felt humiliated or defeated. He provided unconditional love and companionship for hours on end when I was alone in our home and overcome with emotion.

Larry and my children had no idea what was happening in our house when they left for work or school, but Simon knew and it was our secret. The pain I released in his presence and the love he gave me trying to help me heal was our private time. I cherished him.

Nearly a year had passed since I left work and the legal process began. It had been a year of emotional pain and trauma, but also one of physical pain as my broken bone was not healing according to the doctor's expectations. I had already had one surgery and was being troubled by seemingly permanent nerve damage causing pins and needles and weakness in my arm.

I left my home early one morning for my appointment with Dr. Z, sessions I more commonly refer to as "my tune-ups" since they seem to keep me functioning until the next appointment. I failed to notice that as I left my home that a van began to follow me. By the time I had driven about eight miles of the 40-mile ride, the van began to repeatedly honk behind me and the driver was trying to motion for me to pull over. I became quite concerned that perhaps something was wrong with my car, but had no intentions of pulling over for a stranger. I continued to drive and tried to ignore the van, but the driver remained persistent and with the first opportunity pulled up along the right side of my car and held a sign on the window that said, "I'll see you in court."

I had no idea what was happening, but panic began to take over as a surge of adrenaline washed through my body. My entire body began to shake uncontrollably. I was a short distance from Dr. Z's office and all I could think to do was get to his office where I would be safe. For the next hour, Dr. Z calmed me down and strongly recommended that I leave his office and contact the authorities.

I spent a few hours in the local police station trying to explain what I had just experienced and trying further to help them to understand that I was in a very unfortunate legal issue. The police made the required reports and sent me home suggesting that I be more careful of people in my surroundings and to call them if anything else happened. By the time I got home, I was emotionally drained. I was frightened and desperately fearful that my family might be in harm's way as a result of the progression of my legal action.

I let Simon out to relieve himself, unattended for just a few minutes. Less than an hour later, he collapsed in our home and began to suffer and die. Quite literally, one minute he was energetic and happy and the next he was dying. Larry and I rushed him to the vet and no obvious explanation became of his death at that moment. Our otherwise healthy and active dog fell down and died within hours of a van being seen on my street that followed me for several miles to intimidate me. I have my theory as to what happened. Simon is gone and nothing will bring him back.

With Simon's untimely and suspicious death, a part of me died as well. His death thrust me further into the darkness and despair. I was drowning. It was nearly one year to the day after I had left my job. The grieving made it difficult for me to inhale.

I felt responsible for Simon's death and I desperately missed the unconditional devotion he had given me each day that he was part of our family. My grief counselor and private confidante was gone. My once private grieving with only Simon as my witness had become uncontrollably in the open as my husband and children learned to endure my grief. My children were also suffering from the pain of losing their dear friend and childhood pet.

The Poltergeist was being fueled by the emotional suffering, pain, heartbreak and loss and I was the epicenter.

The only other time I can recall such a time of complete loneliness is when Devin was abducted. It was during this time that I think I felt the most defeated. I realized that I was up against an evil force that pretended to regard life as precious, but was willing to meet its own needs regardless of the cost. Struggling to try and remain supportive Larry remained silent but effective with hugs. I knew he was hurting watching me suffer. He loves me. But, he needed to keep the family moving forward. He allowed me my time to fall apart and kept life in motion for himself and our children. My hero on so many levels.

The first year of isolation had passed and Simon had passed as well. I always thought my home was a sanctuary, a sacred space, a safe place to relax and just be.

Instead, my home had become a tomb, an above ground structure that maintained my isolation and my silence as the legal process dragged on with no end in sight. No legal representative or company executive asked to hear my truth. There was paper correspondence, but each time my attorney offered for me to speak, offers were declined.

My depression soon progressed to despair. My private sessions to which Simon had once been silent witness had unwillingly become public as my children and my husband watched me, helpless to know what to do. No one could heal my pain nor could they soothe me through gentle words or hugs. I was inconsolable.

Yes, it was the loss of Simon, but it was something more. I knew I was losing myself.

As I embarked on my second year of isolation, I turned more inwardly to prayer. I began to process and critically evaluate from my childhood forward the connection of my religious experiences and how they contributed to who I had become.

I had very few memories of my childhood or my previous marriage. It seemed that once I overcame those challenges, I closed the doors forever on many of those memories. Yes, I had complete clarity on my childhood abuses and my son's abduction. Certain painful exits on my life's roadmap remained clear, but in my despondency it seemed that my religious experiences, good and bad, were being brought forth in my consciousness to direct me and maybe, just maybe, to heal me.

CHAPTER 17

My Shadow Review

I was born and raised Roman Catholic, so Catholicism was my childhood foundation. It spoke to me through my developmental years. I attended Catholic school where I received a sound private education that in the 1970s far surpassed our local public elementary schools. However, the emotional damage that came with the antiquated parochial tradition caused a different layer of harm.

My school was primarily attended by the upper middle-class children. I was one of two poor children in a class of eighteen students. We were together from kindergarten through eighth grade with little variation in class size along the way. Being poor is not easy, but being poor and being constantly reminded of it by teachers and nuns was frankly humiliating and intended to be so.

My parents were not benefactors to the church, nor did they participate in the PTA. As a matter of fact, my tuition was paid through my father's physical labor. He was a painter by trade and would barter his painting services as a means to keep his daughters in private school. He painted the church and the rectory during my academic studies at this school. As much as I love him for this wonderful sacrifice, he had no understanding of the emotional scarring that was occurring in that building that he thought provided me and my sister with a protective and nurturing academic and religious environment.

My elementary years are filled with memories of being called hurtful names by the school principal. Sr. C referred to me as "fat" on occasion and one of my classmates frequently called me Ms. Piggy. I can recall favoritism amongst teachers for the children of the wealthiest families and my overwhelming desire to fit in, knowing that I didn't. I hold no ill toward the teachers and admistrators that shamed me because of my social status. What I experienced unfortunately continues as the Shadow of Economic Classism and the widening divide between the top 1% and the poor. I was poor in the 70s. I was temporarily homeless. I knew I was different and I felt shame, but I also felt motivated to overcome poverty and become like my friends. As my Dad had previously preached, financial independence could be mine with a good education. Just education wasn't my perceived escape, not yet. It was the early 80s and I was running from fear of being trapped in my current life, no one ever wanting to love me, and no parental role models. My search for safety brought me to the Evangelical church where I was baptized in the Spirit of the Pentacostal church and full of enthusiasm to begin a new Christian life. Church elders blessed a marriage between me, 17, and Gavin, 23, and the drive from New York to the South began. New husband, fresh start, Bible in hand.

Gavin travelled with a gospel singing group and was gone nearly three weeks a month on a tour bus going state to state. That time was an adventure and I met hundreds of truly lovely and inspirational Christian people who loved God and loved each other. They were innocent people who gave generously of themselves and their paychecks as the donation plate was passed around "for the grace of God" by the group that employed Gavin.

Little did these people know that the money they so freely gave was not always being used for the intentions in which they believed. There were no upcoming trips to the Holy Land or Bible distributions to Third World countries. These generous people were being misled and their faith didn't protect them. My introduction to the Shadow of organized religion. I was astonished. In addition to money improprieties was the multitude of sexual liaisons between band members and their mistresses. Women would join them on the bus when the wives were home and disappear when the wives flew in. It was all routine in their world and seemingly guilt free from my vantage point. Hugging, kissing the mistress then dropping them off at the next stop where the devoted wife joined for the rest of the trip. My early lesson in unscrupulous monetary and relationship practices in a Christian religious group. The Shadow of corruption and infidelity intersects all sects.

I recall Gavin justifying the work being done as good work and making excuses for the deceptions to the churchgoers. Yes, I was naïve. I accepted what was being done and remained quiet, in retrospect, I realize this was just another attempt to "fit in."

Eventually, the band (Gavin's employers) began to complain about my presence at their concerts. It was not because I was disruptive or a distraction to Gavin's work responsibilities, rather it was because they were concerned that I would return to their hometown and share stories with their wives about what I was witnessing. So, my visits were banned. To date, I don't think they ever realized all the misappropriations I had observed during my short tenure of travel in 1985. Gavin was "let go" from this job, no surprise. The group cited financial reasons, however the truth was much uglier.

Within a year, we moved back to New York where I eventually

returned to college and graduated in 1989 as a registered nurse. I will mark this milestone as my initiation into my journey of healing as I began to identify my power within. The early intuitiveness to read another's subtle que's of pain or discomfort. The appreciation for the body-mind-spirit connection and all the wonderful theories that encompass nursing as science and art. In the nursing profession I began to grow. My inner Star began to shine and my hope for a brighter future had opportunity for realization.

Consequently, during this time religion left a bad taste in my mouth. I had witnessed too much blatant disregard for other naïve souls that openly gave of their time and their finances only to be cheated and God wasn't stopping it. I was young and still had much to learn. But not in a church. I stopped attending, stayed away from the Bible and just moved at my own pace. I never stopped believing in God before the Poltergeist in my world generated my crisis of faith. I was not able to shrug off the hypocrisies that became public during the late 80s and 90s which included evangelical leaders like Jim Bakker and Jimmy Swaggart begging for forgiveness because Darkness had infiltrated Gods home. It was even less palatable to hear decades of cover ups regarding the Darkness within the Roman Catholic church as their leaders vigorously labored to diminish sexual transgressions within their organization rather than vindicating all the innocent souls that openly trusted in them and were violated on their journey.

When I search for the Light within organized religion, during my generation, I always begin with the selfless life of Mother Teresa and her devoted commune with the impoverished souls of Calcutta, India. She was my first hero. As early as I can remember, perhaps 7 years old, I recall being treated by my church as "less than" for the very Shadow that Mother Teresa was working tirelessly to bring attention to across the globe. The oppressive Darkness of social injustice which continues and is worse today. I then think of all the other beacons of Light, bright Stars, working for similar issues that motivated them to bring love to all sentient beings. Dr. Martin Luther King, Nelson Mandela, the Dalai Lama, the recently deceased and amazing Representative John Lewis. They are just a small sample of the brilliant Stars that would not allow Shadow to ever stop them on their journeys. They suffered and assimilated their pasts only to learn they were brought here to be of service to others, despite the outcome.

As for the blatant cover up of sexual misconduct of any form, I remain speechless. The Shadow of sexual indecency is wrought with debate over what is defined as decent and what is not. Religion and dogma have interfered with sexuality for as long as the desire for human control has existed. Any sexual mistreatment of minors and adults that is robustly hidden is unconscionable in any setting. There was trust established between the victims and perpetrators that provided opportunity for the mistreatment. Within religious organizations the impropriety is perceived as exponentially more egregious because these are places where faith and trust are most expected. Yet, Darkness exists in all venues and never discriminates. Shadow remains a constant force seeking to cause pain and invalidate any and all work toward a peaceful coexistence. Starseeds begin their journey to serve. They bring love and compassion. However, in their trust they are often violated and deceived. Then through the victimization process comes the guilt and shame because they are the problem. This myriad of Dark, traumatic emotions is the power source of the Shadow.

Today, I have a modicum of hope that within the Roman Catholic church, Pope Francis will shine his Light on that heavy Shadow that continues to scar the tribe he has been anointed to shepherd. I see this issue as his soul's journey. I see Pope Francis as a brilliant Starseed brought to earth to live a humble life of service. He suffered and struggled and had to awaken to his Light as the rest of us do. His humility and his candor balance his work and he is learning to walk a delicate line between the Light of God and Darkness that oppresses humanity. A very delicate line. I have hope that he will illuminate these transgressions so that the healing process for many Starseeds will multiply.

Despite my distaste for organized religion, I did put an effort into attending church and building a foundation for my children. I dabbled with the Presbyterian and Methodist faiths and even bounced back to my old Evangelical church for a few Sunday services. But hypocrisy rested in the back of my mind and I no longer felt I could experience God in the traditional venues.

I do not believe there is one straight path to God, rather I believe the roads are infinite. I credit my spiritual evolution to the nursing profession where I learned early that faith is as individual as the human DNA. That my role as a nurse was to never judge another based on their personal beliefs. I witnessed illness, wellness, birth and death in the multitude of faiths that coexist. It is through the assimilation of each that my spiritual self continues to develop.

I do not offer advice. However, I have become a mentor that shares experiences when asked. My beliefs are very much a hybrid of experience, philosophy, and culture. I honor what my mission and purpose is and gently encourage others to do the same. I do not wish to offend any religion nor do I suggest that each organization is entirely flawed. I simply speak to my experience and how my faith has evolved. This is my soul's journey in this lifetime. The journey which I will not regret.

The good, bad, and ugly are the experiences within our Divine fabric that make us the precious souls we are. The Light that shines across the painful roads of Darkness that will try to break our Spirit but with fortitude will bring wisdom and clarity in the end. The key is to get to the end so that you can celebrate your achievement. Honor the pain for the strength it gave you. Acknowledge your inner Star. Here to shine bright, but not without the obligation of your soul's journey to fight to shine. That is what makes the Starseeds Light so much brighter. The perseverance to learn that remaining in the Shadow of victimhood only strengthens an already troubled planet cloaked in Darkness and struggling itself to shine. Our mighty Gaia.

So, as I have matured as a person, I have also matured in Spirit. I respect all faiths, but for me the best fit is with my one on one connection with the Divine. My ability to communicate with Spirit through meditation and other energy modalities has strengthened me and brought clarity to my mission and purpose. Each Dark road has sought to keep me broken, but each accomplishment brought the return of self-esteem and the return of my Light. Yet, the process isn't always forward motion. Darkness continually tries to create set-backs and self-doubt. That is why it is vitally important to maintain a daily spiritual practice. Light will always be challenged. The duality that pre-dates human existence.

For me, mentorship is part of life's work. Starseeds are in desperate need of compassion and empathy from others because they unselfishly give so much of themselves without regard to how personally draining it may be. My inner Light grew as I fought for my voice and learned the hard way that I cannot serve others if I am not serving myself first. With this statement, I pause. I had to BE my true Light BEFORE I could help others shine. That is what I was born to do. That is why I had so much to overcome. In my suffering, I became stronger. The healer that is my mission and purpose. In the silence of litigation. In the failure of wife and mother. In the pain of womanhood was a Starseed that wanted to shine but had no road map to show me the way. The challenges would continue for a while longer. My lessons continued.

"Mom, I have a stomach ache," I heard one afternoon as Ian joined me on the front porch where I was sitting in the afternoon sun reflecting on my life and the legal drama that consumed my attention along with my fear of failure and letting down my family.

"Where does it hurt, baby?" I asked. I still called him "Baby" sometimes, despite what others may say, even though Ian was eleven years old and my youngest. He will always be Mama's baby. I spent a few minutes assessing his symptoms and gave my expert treatment advice: "Go try to fart and that should make it better."

Of course he agreed, being a young boy and having some experience with this as well as the eleven-year old obsession with humorous bodily processes.

He sat with me for a little bit and tried to shake off the discomfort while we waited for his dad to come home from work. It was the first day of Larry's vacation and we were going to go for a drive and then out to eat. As the sun shone down on a beautiful day, the humidity seemed to be breaking and just a few clouds skipped through the bright blue sky. We waited for Larry's return and that one big fart of relief for Ian's aching stomach.

By early evening, the stomach pain persisted and my little guy was just trying to tolerate it. Recognizing that this was no simple stomach ache, I started assessing him further and began to fear the alternate diagnosis: a hot appendix.

By 5 p.m., I called his doctor and asked if I could bring him for a visit. We are fortunate in our community to have good access to medical care. Our pediatrician's office is open most nights till 8 p.m. and that night we needed to make use of it

As I was on the phone explaining Ian's symptoms to the receptionist, I heard a cry for help coming from the family room. I turned around to see my son just a foot away from the bathroom door, vomiting all over the carpet.

"Damn!" was my first thought. I felt terrible that he was starting to vomit, but of course I was trying to process the situation.

"How am I going to get the vomit off the floor?" I wondered. Hanging up the phone, I led him into the bathroom and simultaneously try to keep our new puppy, Kobe, away from the mess.

"Larry!" I screamed. "I need your help!"

We scrambled to clean the carpet, monitor Ian and prepare to leave for the doctor's office.

"It looks like we have appendicitis." Dr. C calmly broke the news to my squirming son. His eyes opened wide as he fought to hold back his tears. My husband may have been a little bit surprised by the news, but I was already pretty sure of my diagnosis and was making mental preparations for the next step. It took a few more minutes to complete some lab work, followed by a stressful conversation about which hospital to go to.

Pediatric cases in our region often go to a larger medical facility about 100 miles away. Dr. C advised that if it was her child, she would go there. However, I didn't feel comfortable travelling that far. It is an outstanding teaching facility, yet I was unsettled with the thought of the accompanying flood of residents, interns and other various medical students who would be practicing on my son. To add to my dismay, this appendix issue was occurring in the month of July. Rule number one on teaching hospitals: Avoid them in month of July. This is when the influx of new residents takes place and it is statistically when the most patient mistakes occur. So, my inner voice was screaming to me, "Stay local."

Thank God my husband agreed.

Confirmation of appendicitis was completed with a CT scan and two more hours of waiting while Ian writhed in pain. As I sat and watched my son and his hot appendix simmering, I prayed relentlessly that he didn't start to boil. A boil could land us in much more than a routine procedure. Ian was in the operating room by 2:40 a.m. and in the recovery room 40 minutes later. Surgery was textbook smooth. We could exhale and Ian could begin to heal.

Despite my 20 years in the field, the advancements of medicine truly still amaze me. When I first became a nurse, most patients with appendectomies had a hospital stay of about four days. Ian was in the recovery room at 3:30 a.m. and home watching cartoons by 11:30 a.m. I could not have asked for a better outcome. As important as this successful outcome, was my ability to face the irrational fear and anxiety that my child was going to die with a reasonable sense of calm. My faith was returning. God was with my child and he was going to be okay.

CHAPTER 18

I Am Light

As the years of isolation continued, my family demonstrated more resolve than I did. Devin grew up and prepared for a semester abroad of study. My other boys excelled in school and sports while Larry kept steering the ship. I watched my family grow and develop and continued in my silent vigil, my Shadow tomb, awaiting my day in court so I could speak my truth. Trying to understand how I got to this surreal place in life.

My consistent therapy with Dr. Z led to a diagnosis of Post-Traumatic Stress Disorder (PTSD). PTSD is a phenomenon that may occur as a result of some unforeseen trauma. It is more common in people with underlying anxiety and past trauma. I have always acknowledged and respected the disorder and its devastating effect it can have on people. However, I had never thought of myself as being a potential victim of such a disorder. In my mind, PTSD is reserved for military personnel and victims of tragic events such as rape. But, the behaviors I was exhibiting were consistent with my diagnosis despite my reluctance to accept it.

I had reached my lowest point. Larry was reporting to Dr. Z and me the erratic and irrational behavior that I was exhibiting. There were things I wasn't recognizing I was doing. I would fly off the handle at the simplest stressors. I was not sleeping. I was crying all the time in front of my children. I was distancing myself from my immediate family, not returning phone calls and generally avoiding contact with others. Although, Larry was trying to remain patient and explain to me that I was not acting appropriately, I would become more hostile toward him and accusatory. I told him many times that he was unsympathetic and judgmental. It sucked.

From the depths of this Darkness, it was a routine physical with my long-time primary care physician that shined early Light and set the wheels of healing in motion. He recommended a meeting with a wonderful spiritual counselor and gave me her contact information.

I called Claire and scheduled a meeting with a renewed sense of hope. We never discussed details of my legal action. We focused our visits on strengthening my spiritual foundation, meditation techniques and energy balancing through Reiki.

Claire helped me to reconnect with my higher self, my intuitive knowing. It was through this teaching that my personal trust began to grow. I learned how to listen to and communicate with my higher self. I learned meditation and began the important process of journeling my experiences during meditation. I began to develop my own ways to self-heal and begin to experience all the spiritual energy around us. Sitting in nature and tuning all my senses help to awaken my intuition and communication with other Light energies. I began to recognize my need to forgive on different levels as a means to truly reclaim me.Our new puppy, Kobe brought restored the energy of unconditional love in my life. It is incredible how a two-pound Bichon no bigger than Ian's sneaker could begin to refill my soul. Kobe brought instant joy to all of us after had had suffered so much with the loss of Simon, but for me Kobe had a more profound purpose: He was my new angel, another gift from the Divine intended to teach me about the Star I am and how precious each soul is. I could love and nurture and watch this new little life grow and learn during a time when I felt withered and barren.

Embarking on this new path, I learned the importance of daily meditation to ground and balance myself as a method of preparing for what the day may bring. To sit in silence and clear my thoughts for five minutes was difficult. Learning how to empty an unnaturally cluttered mind is a process that requires patience, but it is important, and it works. We are energetic beings, surrounded and infused by energy. Our Light is energy and so is our Dark. Consider the calories we consume and the means required to burn them. Calories are our fuel, energy. Exercise the energetic means by which we burn our fuel. The this concept out a bit further and consider the energy of the world we live in, natural and man-made. Lightening from which pre-civilized fire and industrial age electricity was discovered. Simple bread mold from which antibiotics were discovered. Natural energies that when combined with the initiative of humankind changed the paths for civilizations. But, energy and matter have a beginning. Some of us believe that this beginning is The Divine/God/The Source… and all energy is part of the universal matrix that is Divine.

Our best opportunity, perhaps at minimum our best first step, to connect our energy with the Divine is through the practices of meditation, prayer, and mindfulness. In the steps of these practices we learn to slow down our chaotic energy and attune our senses to the energies that surround us. We can experience the energetic bond rather than just speak about it. We can recharge our Light. It seems too simple in our complex world, but God didn't create all the complexities we did. Think of how refreshing it is to take time out and be in nature. A hike in the woods, a day by the ocean, a drive in the mountains. Nature and human are creations of the Divine and when we combine our energies and shut off the chatter we return to a place of peace. We begin to restore and replenish.

Our world is moving in a frenzy of chaotic energy that can be disorienting. Societal shadows want us to remain cloudy and ineffective. Maintaining a lifestyle where we feel there is "never enough time" is part of the Shadow plan to keep us disconnected. So many problems are easily improved, not necessarily solved, but improved if people would stop saying, "I don't have the time". Obesity, hypertension, anxiety disorder, marital and child rearing issues always seem to have a component of lack of time within the very issue being addressed. In truth, we do have time but Shadow wants us to remain distracted and chaotic because the power remains in the Darkness. Individual and societal healing is reliant on our ability to connect with the collective consciousness of Light that is Divine. To slow down our pace, take five minutes back each day, and connect with the Divine to reclaim the power of everything that is important to you. Before you realize, five minutes will become 10 and you will realize that your world hasn't crumbled in those 10 restorative minutes. Quite the opposite occurs. The Shadow and repetitive patterns that are harmful are being weakened because your energy is learning to feel peace. It is learning to trust. And your Star within is beginning to shine. Each of us needs to listen to our little voices more openly and honor our Star within. We need to trust our instincts like our lives depend on it because they do.

Each day when I begin my meditation, I state my clear intention for the day. I am an active participate in how my day will proceed. I offer gratitude for all the upcoming opportunities including my ability to give back to the world in my healing role. This is a tremendous blessing that I never take for granted.

I prepare myself by turning on my energetic Light brightly and asking my Spirit guides to help me navigate the Shadows that may try to block my path. My intention each and every day is "to know my En-Lightened nature that I may benefit all beings." I am the creator of my journey, but I know I will experience challenges that I must learn to overcome. Each day will bring varying degrees of Shadow, but today I am better equipped because I consciously connect with the Divine. Today I understand and participate with all sentient beings to be part of the healing process, a positive contributor to the greater good.

Through my ongoing spiritual work and continued therapy with Dr. Z, I became much more perceptive to the patterns of dysfunction from my past and the similarities in my present. But understanding and recognizing patterns does not eliminate the emotions that these patterns invoke in my being.

I was able to re-frame past resentments as I now interpret my challenges through a clearer lens. Anger and resentment toward my mother diffused. Acknowledgement of her manipulative and deceptive behaviors was no longer painful to manage. I know longer blamed myself for being born and ruining her life. I became able to openly send my mother love without condition and compassion during her soul's journey.

The years I spent blaming myself for Devin's abduction were being re-framed. I believed that if I hadn't hurt Gavin, then he wouldn't have hurt me. This was flawed thinking. Gavin was unable to accept that I didn't love him and didn't want to be married to him. As a result of his poor coping skills, he manipulated me into staying with him and caused unspeakable trauma to our son through his abduction. Rather than accepting and coming to terms with what could have been an amicable divorce, he chose to manipulate me more by taking my son from me. The message he was sending was, "if I can't have you then you can't have Devin." This is supported by the fact that Gavin gave me back my son when he thought I had returned to our marriage. Unfortunately, the consequence of his poor choice has to this day cost Gavin his relationship with his son.

Steve let me know that if I continued my pregnancy against his wishes, then I was on my own. It was a shameful situation for me to overcome, but he could not manipulate my behavior this time.

I spent the majority of my lifetime being manipulated and conversely learning how to manipulate. My mother was a strong role model for manipulative behavior and I learned well. With Larry, it wasn't that he was manipulating me; it was the opposite. I had become so full of my own ego and inflated personal expectations that I manipulated him to get what I wanted. As a result, our marriage nearly crumbled and I nearly lost the most important person in my life.

In my forced isolation, I turned to prayer. I prayed for direction. I prayed for healing. I prayed for strength for my family, my patients, but most importantly, I began to pray for those who had caused me harm. The Shadow of isolation forced me into an intense exploration into the whys and hows of my life. I have heard that out of our Darkest moments can come the most brilliant Light if we choose to do the work required to gain understanding.

When my body broke, literally during a delivery, it was the beginning of my journey toward my inner Light. Darkness and despondency tried to root themselves and create destruction of myself and my family.

My faith was challenged, nearly destroyed. But nearly is the
key word that requires deeper evaluation. How many times during
my childhood, adolescence, young adulthood and adulthood was
my faith tested? Was I nearly destroyed? It seemed that all those
life lessons were manifesting into one physical break that was
preparing me for my ultimate test.

Loss of a career, shattering of my ego, failure of my family…
I never could have imagined the personal and spiritual growth
that would follow. I never would have imagined that I could
reach such a personal low moment and still have the resolve to
overcome and become a better person than when I started.

That is the journey of the Starseed. And it is hard work.
Sometimes it is more work than I want it to be. But now when I
feel discouraged it only takes a few moments for me to re-frame
my personal struggle into a challenge that can be overcome. I
take time to consider all the souls around me and the Shadows
they may be experiencing and how mine may be very insignificant
compared to another's. Through all the trauma, much extraor-
dinary, to give up and scream victim would give victory to the
Shadow. This I cannot do.

I had much to process and as I developed the steps that work
for me and it became apparent that each of us is a victim at times,
but each of us is also a perpetrator. Duality again reflected in
human behavior. I cannot excuse the choices I have made that
caused harm to others because I was a victim. It was because I
was a victim that I also learned how to become a perpetrator.
The cycle of manipulation that is often repeated because we are
unable to clear our path and consciously choose to change our
patterns despite how hard it may be.

I was in physical pain every day from my injury, which still
had not completely healed, but had not yet been classified as

permanent. A local newspaper had printed an article about my legal action without regard for my privacy. I had been followed by a strange vehicle, buried my dog and continued to be flabbergasted by a legal process that would lose a race with a snail. After all that had transpired, the call from my attorney finally came. "Stacey your deposition is scheduled."It was time. No further witnesses to be called. No more witnesses that "did not recall". My deposition would mark the ending of the preliminary proceedings then we would learn if my case would be scheduled for trial. Time to speak my truth.

I had never been deposed before, but my attorney had forewarned me that I would leave the event feeling like the rape victim who was to blame because her skirt was "too short."

This is not a far-off analogy. It was grueling, humiliating and exhausting. After this experience, I can understand how an innocent person might confess to murder after the nine hours of questioning like I endured. I was made to feel like I was the perpetrator rather than the victim. To say that the defense attorneys treated me like shit doesn't do them justice for just how low they can sink.

I was trained in nursing. In nursing, it is my utmost goal and priority to help my patient. Nursing and law are polar opposites.

In nursing, we are trained in the art and science of healing and to cause no harm. This is termed non-maleficence.

The attorneys were being paid to do whatever it took to win the case. Victory at whatever cost. They were going to cause harm in order to protect their client, guilty or not, culpable or not. The attorneys were not concerned with my emotional or physical state. Non-maleficence is not in the lawyer's vocabulary. It was all about the win, regardless of the damage.

Before this day came, I called on Judy, one of my closest

friends and mentors, and asked her to lead a prayer circle to help strengthen my spirit before I faced the defending attorneys.

My sister attended the prayer circle, along with a small group of friends that who had no idea I was involved in a lawsuit until the local newspaper printed my story. Remember my attorneys had imposed a strict order of silence on me. The prayer circle gathered at my home a few days before my deposition. I am still overwhelmed with joy at the love and support my friends showed me. A prayer circle puts forth the request of the person who requests it. I was seeking a time of prayer and an immersion in the positive love energy of friendship. Judy led the circle with her unique spiritual wisdom and guided me through the process. The day before I was deposed with the love of my tribal sisters and before God I affirmed my intention to:

HONOR MY VOICE

SPEAK MY TRUTH

OVERCOME FEAR

AND MAINTAIN CLARITY

As the prayer circle ended, I felt blanketed in love, filled with strength and ready to face any Darkness that would come my way. I was grateful for the support of women that had known me for a lifetime but had just learned of the silent suffering I had been enduring. I felt special that they would make time in their busy lives to pray for me.

On the day of the deposition, my attorney reinstructed me to wait for the question to be asked in its entirety before I answered and to answer only the question asked. It sounded simple, but it was not easy. Two years had passed, and this would be the first time anyone involved with my former employer was going to hear my truth. My biggest fear was that from the first moment I could finally speak, I might not be able to stop. I did my best.

Despite the opposing attorneys' best effort to get me to fumble my story. I stood firm. I cried hysterically at times. I yelled back a little bit. They tried their best to demean and humiliate me. But I stood firm. The attorneys broke for a late lunch and returned to grill me for three more hours. My inquisition ended and I was drained.

As part of the demoralizing process, the attorney's found it important to have me state, on the record, that that I don't wear panties. Yes, it is true. It was not a secret then and is part of the legal record now. My personal choice to not wear undergarments was used as a weapon against me. It was insinuated to be some sort of defective risqué behavior and they used it to try to discredit me. Somehow my admission that I do not wear panties was a way to excuse Roger's harassment or my employer's responsibility to have acted more expeditiously. To put this in simpler terms, they were arguing that I was to blame because it was known that I don't wear panties, therefore any sexual harassment was my fault. If I wore panties, maybe this wouldn't have happened. Victim blaming front and center.

Nine hours of questioning was finally over. I was raw, emotionally drained and shattered from the repeated accusation that I brought Roger's behavior on myself. That was just how the opposing attorneys wanted me to feel. Nevertheless, I had stood up to the accusations and defended my position. No matter what, I spoke my truth. Depositions of all witnesses lasted for several more months with all questioning ending two and one-half years after I left my job. Roger remained employed. I continued to endure physical and emotional damage.

During a woman's labor process, when the fetal head begins to stretch and thin the perineum in preparation for the inevitable delivery, there is an intense fiery burning sensation. This burning sensation is unlike any other pain described during an injury. The relentless pressure of the fetal head stretching open the vagina from finger-width to the width of a full size baby's head creates hyperactive nerve impulses that rapidly transmit this fiery hot sensation that can make a woman feel like she is being ripped in two. This experience has long been identified as, "the ring of fire."

One of my spiritual mentors, Helena, called my painful, surreal experience in the nine hours of deposition my own personal "ring of fire." Despite the lawyers' taunting, the accusations that I deserved Roger's unwelcome attentions and their efforts to make me feel like a whore, I survived.

Unquestionably, I was battered by the experience, but I survived.

CHAPTER 19

The Forgiveness Factor

Spiritual growth is unique to each individual's belief system. There is no single right or wrong way to approach spirituality. The prayer and meditation that I developed reflects my cultural background along with the guidance of my spiritual mentors who entered my life during my crisis.

Some days are better than others, but I have not had a miraculous healing. The Shadows are always present and there are days they can wreak more havoc and test my mettle. I am Starseed, but I am living a human life. As a human, I am prone to the dualities of victimhood vs perpetrator like all others. I have been both.

My soul is Light and requires recharging by the modalities that I have learned to help protect me from the Darkness of my past and the challenges in the present. This is the process of the human journey. We are here to learn and grow.

Integral to our search is to identify our mission and purpose. What resonates with you and sustains you on your daily journey? I am a healer. My professional career has been decades of caring for others. This truth is despite not being able to properly nurture myself. I am trained to assess, diagnose, and treat illness. I am trained to prevent illness.

But that training did not translate in my personal life. Eventually, my lack of self-care caught up to me. I broke physically and emotionally. I needed to learn how to bring the missing pieces of me back together so that I could continue in this life more whole as I resumed the journey of my mission and purpose. My personal goal is to attain my enlightened self before this life ends. My life's work is to continue to heal myself and heal others. Each not mutually exclusive more clearly revealed during my years in the Shadows of isolation, shame, and guilt.

By the year three of being entombed, I was encouraged to return to college and earn yet another degree. Midwifery, my passion, was no longer an option given the hand injury that was not completely healing. This proved to be a significant part of my suffering, the loss of the job that I had wanted since I was a young child. The fact that I was forced into leaving, no option offered, added to my grief. I had academic options since I appreciatively learn easily. If I apply myself I will succeed, so my choice was to earn a doctorate in public health, a program that would challenge my mind and enrich my nursing background.

Studies were a welcome distraction. I had nothing else that would distract me from the painfully long process of awaiting the decision from the court. Would I be granted the right to a trial or not? That was the long-awaited answer upon review of all depositions by the judge.

Most ordinary people don't realize, I certainly didn't, that just because a lawsuit is started does not guarantee a day in court. My legal action was in federal court, not state court, and the rules of each are vastly different. During the stressful wait, I was offered financial settlement to end the case, but as I have always maintained money wasn't my motivator. My reputation mattered. I believed that a jury of my peers should be the arbiters of my case. Money wasn't going to heal my wounds

Legal closure came abruptly when the court decided that

I was not entitled to a trial. The decision cited that I had not reported one year from the first incident that I perceived was inappropriate, therefore I had failed to report within the statute of limitations. My attorney and other legal professionals had believed that the court would not interpret the timing of reporting as from the first incident, but rather from the last incident. However, this federal court judge didn't see it that way. She ruled against me leaving the option of accepting loss or filing an appeal to the NYS 2nd Circuit Court Southern District. I was already living in a state of perpetual numbness. My attorney believed that an appeal was a reasonable option. Larry chose to defer from sharing any opinion and respect whatever I felt was right for me.

You see, the legal system by design does not consider human emotions and the fact that victims feel powerless and time is needed not only to find the courage to report, but often to identify the wrongdoing. Victims are not processing their abuse within a framework of a legal statute of limitations, rather they are just struggling to survive. A one-year time limit the judge imposed on my suffering seemed incredibly unfair to me, but I had yet to learn that it is unfair to most victims of workplace harassment.

I chose to file in the court of appeals, but at the same time I chose the topic for my doctoral dissertation. I was going to conduct research on workplace harassment in nursing. It was what I was enduring and in my very core I believed that something was painfully wrong with this assigned statute of limitations for victims.

The next two years were a whirlwind of healing energy for me. My Light began to glow and I was reinventing myself through my doctoral studies and my healing practices. Before I graduated, I did have the opportunity to stand in the Southern District Court of Appeals in lower Manhattan. I was before three esteemed federal judges and absolutely in awe of the process of law as it revealed in my case. Timers on and each side given just minutes to defend their position or take questions from the panel of judges.

I maintained guarded hope that we may overturn the previous judgment, but in the end I lost. It wasn't that my truth was doubted, it was that I failed to report within the legal statute of limitations. With that my story would end. I had no emotional strength to seek justice in our country's Supreme Court. That was going to have to be a fight for a different victim. Perhaps then, my lawsuit would be cited and the law to protect victims changed. But for me, I was tired of the fight.

The Shadow was immense. It was hateful and it enjoyed laughing at me with every tear I shed. I'm often asked if I regretted not settling before the judge's initial decision and I respectfully respond, "It was never about money."

I was born without money and, if for nothing else, I knew I would always be able to provide for myself. This legal action was about defending myself against a predator who was much bigger than me.

In my naivete, I didn't think the legal process could be so painful. I never thought it would be so protracted and isolating. I never thought I had a sure win, but I never thought I would be denied a trial. So, with the decision behind me and research deadlines closing in, my pilot study began with a fury.

I was contacted by nearly 90 nurses across the United States who learned about my study and wanted to participate. They had a story, too. They had been victimized, too. The overwhelming majority never reported to their superiors. The overwhelming majority took at least nine months before they were able to identify the mistreatment as harassment.

OMG! I was not alone! Victims are delayed in coming to terms with their experiences. Nearly 90 nurses spoke to this point. Therefore, the law doesn't seem to support a victim's timeline. This knowledge alone, even though it is early data, offered me profound healing from a Shadow of demoralization of the legal process.

I heard stories from brave nurses who trusted me and felt validated fully knowing this was a simple pilot study; these were preliminary findings. They were open and grateful. I honor them for braveness. These nurses helped me heal. They are my heroes. The data they provided supports a need for re-consideration of the reporting mandates of our antiquated federal workplace protection laws. Each of these nurses also lived in the Shadow and many endured feelings of shame and isolation. Some left the nursing profession as a result and some still worked in the place where they continue to be mistreated.

The law didn't protect me, but the cumulative experiences bestowed me with a Post-Traumatic Stress Disorder diagnosis. That is a Shadow that I have learned to manage but have yet to fully recover. A powerful Shadow that can be triggered without warning, reminding me that I am a Starseed, a child of Light, but I remain a fragile human. I am still vulnerable at times. The greatest strength comes from the steps I developed toward self-healing that include the power of forgiveness and different energetic modalities which I use daily to strengthen myself body, mind, and spirit.

Forgiveness is essential to healing. Many victims do not like to consider this because they translate forgiveness defeat.

I respectfully and profusely disagree. Anger, rage, anxiety, expectations of apologies, etc., create dis-ease in our bodies, body, mind, and spirit. Stomach aches, headaches, nausea, depression can be manifestations of holding on to the multitude of Shadows that have created pain in your life. An expectation of forgiveness by another only provides fuel for the manifestations of symptoms that you may experience. Forgiveness is the power. Releasing the energy of the Shadow through forgiveness is not a concession to defeat. Releasing the energy of the Shadow is the fuel necessary to empower you. Forgiveness provides a release of all the manifestations of illness related to the Shadows and allows your Light to infuse your body, mind, and spirit with healing. Forgiveness is a process that cannot be rushed, especially if it feels counterintuitive to you when considered. I posit that it is easier to hate than it is to forgive. Most people will agree with me. But, significant personal healing is best achieved through the power of forgiveness.

"*The Forgiveness Factor*" contains the steps I developed during my spiritual journey toward healing. Each one was as necessary as the next. None of them kept a specific order. As Shadows that I needed to clear presented, I would choose the best step to help reach that goal. Different steps in forgiveness address different places of pain. Holistic healing is comprehensive and respects our need to shine our Light physically, emotionally, and spiritually.

First, is the ability to forgive another for the hurt that has been caused. This is accomplished by consciously identifying the hurt, acknowledging the lesson it has brought, then developing the ability to release that hurt, no longer harboring it within one's being. For me, I systematically and painstakingly itemized the hurt I felt from childhood to the present and thanked each hurtful moment for the lessons I learned. Forgiveness was possible when I released the hurt because it no longer served a purpose.

The next type of forgiveness is the recognition that we may

cause pain to others and releasing the personal pain that comes from the pain I have caused. I caused Larry so much pain over the years and owning this was tremendously difficult. I had manipulated and lied as I sought personal gratification at the expense of my partner. I needed to acknowledge that I caused him pain so that I could offer a sincere apology. But there is another Shadow that presents when you acknowledge you have disrespected another. It is the Shadow that prevents us from loving ourselves without condition. We all make mistakes and as we seek forgiveness from others so must we forgive ourselves. Forgiving myself proved to be more challenging than being forgiven by my husband.

In the steps of *The Forgiveness Factor*, you begin by journaling the whats, whys, and hows you believe are important on your healing path. In a simple journal, begin to list the Shadows that surround you. Include all people, emotions, and experiences. If it is preventing you from being your Light then it warrants a deeper look:

1. Identify the people who have caused me pain and why I feel this pain.

2. Identify the pain I feel from others and consciously release it to the universe in a personal ritual.

3. Allow myself to forgive those who have caused me pain as a means to my physical, emotional and spiritual healing.

4. Identify the people I have caused pain and why I caused pain.

5. Identify the pain that I caused others with my actions.

6. Allow myself forgiveness for the pain I have caused others as a means to my physical, emotional and spiritual healing.

It's not easy to forgive others for the pain or hurt that they have intentionally caused. Human nature steps in and wants to interfere with the forgiveness process. The Old Testament speaks of, "an eye for an eye." Most of us can identify with that. But then Jesus came along in the New Testament and undid retaliation and spoke of "turning the other cheek." Jesus' philosophy is far less palatable in terms of human nature's desire for revenge for perceived wrongs. Yet, by allowing positive energy to flow throughout my being without impediment, I learned to release hurt caused by others and become open to the idea of forgiveness. For me, learning how to forgive family members and past relationships was vital to my healing.

Each step is systematic and with intent to heal. Take the time to follow them and repeat as necessary. Identifying Shadow pain, people that caused it and then finding personal power in the lessons you learned brings power back to you. It validates your story and makes it easier to release the pain because not it is understood, and it is no longer needed.

Next, consciously label the feelings, write sentences or paragraphs, and read them. Sit with them for a moment to thank the lessons before releasing it to the universe. Write on paper and burn the paper in your personal ceremony sending the pain out to the universe to be healed by the Divine. Blow the ashes away if you would like and dance and release any pent-up energy around those feelings. This process of ritualistic release of the pain, rage and fear made is empowering and helps closure to begin.

These steps toward are based on my belief that I am an energetic being. I self-identify as a Starseed, a soul whose beginnings come from deep within the belly of the universe. A star system that requires no outward identification because the simple admission is outlandish enough to most. As an energetic being, I consider the duality of Light vs Dark as a paradigm that pre-dates humanity. I further posit that all sentient beings are challenged within this Light vs Dark paradigm and it is part of our pre-determined soul's journey to fight through the trials good, bad, and ugly.

Many humans feel disconnected in today's Shadowy existence. They feel out of place. They feel like they don't belong and they feel like life is too dark and too cruel. Many humans feel overcome by Darkness and are not sure how to manage. Each soul reading this message who craves Light—which I will loosely define as love, peace, kindness, compassion, gentleness—may consider that they to have a connection with Star energy. I will suggest that if it feels right, then it is right. Consequently, if it feels wrong, it isn't right.

From the day of our birth, we become a daughter or son. We grow in our families, our tribes and develop according to their particular belief systems. Some of us feel complete in this system and others will alter or modify according to what feels right for them.

Many of us follow along the path in an orderly fashion trying to assimilate with the status quo, while others can't seem to fit in. Something isn't right. That something is not yet defined. And so they may choose to self-identify outside of the tribe, to march to their own beat and accept the criticism or rejection that may be part of their choice. Others will dabble in different options seeking and maybe getting closer, but not feeling like they found it yet, whatever *it* is.

It is the human journey that brings us to our endpoint. One day we will reach completion in this body and likely reflect on the roads we chose. But till that final day arrives, it is important to consider the power of you and whether you believe your power is here to be of service or to cause harm. It is in that answer that you will be able to best consider where you align with Light vs Dark. If you choose Light then expect challenges from the Shadow for the rest of your life. Yet, don't fear the Shadows despite how oppressive they can be. Utilize the tools available to maintain your energetic strength. Seek a mentor that can assist you in your spiritual journey. Don't demonstrate fear, but have a healthy respect for what you don't yet know.

Along my journey I have faced many Shadows, including direct assaults on my character more than once. My Spirit was broken a few times and my Light went out along the way. My power was restored and my Light recharged when I faced the Demons head on. No time for fear. My energetic self was refueled and I was learning that I am a force to be reckoned with.

I am a Starseed. I am a healer. My mission and purpose is to serve others and help them along their journeys. I trust in the Divine and I am surrounded by Angels and Ascended Masters that are here to protect all sentient beings. I will no longer give my power to another being or another situation. It may be said that I spent most of my life being a victim in some regard, but no more.

I am in control now. I went through the ring of fire and birthed myself anew. Yes, there are some significant burns and scars, but today I have been tempered like steel. Today I am a wiser and more powerful woman. Today, I can honor my inner Star and look toward the future with confidence and strength. I no longer wear a mask to hide my shame. I embrace the true person I am. I help those that seek guidance do the same.

Message
from the Author

Since the end of my legal action, several women have come forward openly to share their personal stories of sexual harassment and victimization in the workplace. #metoo is a powerful force that began to shine Light on the abuse of perpetrators. Social media was important to the movement because victims received support from others and learned they were not the only ones. My story pre-dates #metoo and through the many years of isolation I did feel like I was the only one. It was a lonely road. My healing was reinforced through continuation of my graduate studies earning a doctorate in public health. My research was on sexual harassment and bullying in nursing. I heard many stories of nurses that had similar experiences to mine, some worse. I learned that this phenomenon was much more prevalent in healthcare and I was indeed not alone.

To every victim, I honor you and your experience. I send love and visualize you releasing the heavy grey fog of fear, shame, anxiety. I see it breaking apart into pieces and scattering into the wind. Shadow being carried away never to be seen again. Then, this brilliant shimmering white energy gently cocoons you with love, safety, and security. You feel strange with such a feeling of calm because your world has been chaotic for so long. But this gentle Light speaks to your intuition and tells you the pain is gone. The time has come to let go of the Shadow that prevents you from shining your inner Light. The time has come for you to love every piece of you. Picture all your pieces coming back together as this brilliant white Light becomes the energetic glue that gently restores you to wholeness, your separate pieces once again return to their rightful place.

A new beginning. A fresh start.

Blessings, Stacey

Made in the USA
Middletown, DE
11 November 2023